400 Fascinating Magic Tricks You Can Do

Howard Thurston

Melvin Powers
Wilshire Book Company

12015 Sherman Road, No. Hollywood, CA 91605

Printed in the United States of America
ISBN 0-87980-257-X

INTRODUCTION

This book has been designed to provide the reader with a large variety of magic tricks that can be performed with ordinary articles and which require only a slight amount of practice. It thus gives the beginner an immediate introduction to magic, while the advanced student will find its pages filled with workable material to which he can constantly refer.

The tricks themselves consist of those selected by Howard Thurston, the famous magician, who made a specialty of gathering such material over many years. His experience proved that persons who took up magic as a hobby soon learned to appreciate the art of the professional magician; hence the ever-increasing interest in magic can be directly attributed to the groundwork established in this volume.

For convenience and quick reference, this book has been divided into alphabetical chapters according to the types of objects used in the different tricks. The reader will find occasional cross-references from one section to another and many adaptations will suggest themselves as he proceeds with his study of the magical methods involved.

It has long been said that the best way to learn magic is to begin doing it and "400 Tricks You Can Do" will enable anyone to fulfill that aim. Simply find the type of trick you would like to do, try it, and when the result is satisfactory, proceed with others of your choice. This will lead to the gradual building of a repertoire of magic that can be constantly replenished with new items.

INTRODUCTION

There is nothing difficult about performing magic, as skill is not the primary factor involved. The object of the magician is to mystify and this is best done by applying subtle methods which are thoroughly elucidated in this volume. In fact, some of the simplest tricks are the best, provided of course that proper measures are taken to conceal that very simplicity. As a result, presentation is a highly important factor. Every trick should be presented as though it were a great mystery and this in itself is half the fun of magic.

Certain rules are very valuable as they are practicable with almost all tricks. One good rule is never to tell your audience what you intend to do before you do it. Not anticipating the result, they are unable to catch any advance clues to the climax, which will come as a great and effective surprise.

Similarly, it is unwise to perform the same trick twice on one occasion. Obviously, to repeat a trick is to give advance knowledge of the climax. Here, however, the magician has an excellent surprise weapon at his command. There are many tricks which appear alike, but are actually dependent upon different methods and sometimes produce an unexpected conclusion. Thus in response to the request of "do it again" the magician can often switch to another trick that will seem to be a repetition but will actually provide a new mystery.

Above all, do not explain a trick after you have done it. That simply breaks down the mystery and causes people to lose interest in your magic. The best policy is to proceed with another trick, because when people want to know how a trick is done, it proves they are in a mood to be further mystified. Of course there are certain tricks, more in the puzzle class than strictly magic, which can occasionally be divulged to inquisitive spectators. A considerable number of these are included in this volume and will be easily recognized as such when the reader comes across them.

Certain tricks are appropriate for certain occasions and the best way to ascertain this is by experiment with the tricks them-

INTRODUCTION

selves. Therefore the performer should study the effect of each trick upon his audience in order to learn which is the most effective. Results vary with the performer as well as with the audience, hence there are two rules to cover this. One is, you should like a trick before you try to do it; the other rule is to make sure that it is the sort of trick that your particular audience will like. This again merely emphasizes the importance of observing audience reactions to your magic.

Your talk or "patter" is important and should be rehearsed along with the method of a trick. This is something which depends a great deal upon the individual, particularly where small magic is concerned. To a degree, your style should be strictly natural, since you are performing impromptu magic; nevertheless, there is often an opportunity to build up interest by attributing your tricks to some phenomenal ability which you have acquired. This again is a matter of experience, plus observation of audience reactions.

Suggestions for patter are given with some of the tricks in this book and will serve as guides to others, but in most instances it will be found that the line of talk will develop along with the trick itself. This is much better than attempting to memorize and rehearse an artificial speech which may not be suited to your own particular style of presentation.

In preparing this edition of "400 Tricks You Can Do" the chapters have been rearranged and much of the material has been revised, with the inclusion of some new and effective items. For ready reference, the table of contents lists all the tricks in numerical order, under their respective chapter headings.

CONTENTS

CONTENTS

CONTENTS

CONTENTS

CONTENTS

CONTENTS

CONTENTS

CONTENTS

CHAPTER I

BALL TRICKS

1. THE APPEARING BALL

The magician shows the palm of his hand, absolutely empty. He reaches in the air, and catches a wooden ball at his finger tips.

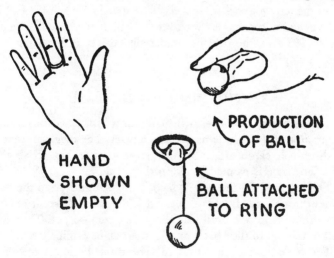

HAND SHOWN EMPTY

PRODUCTION OF BALL

BALL ATTACHED TO RING

A ring must be worn on the second finger of the right hand. A thread about an inch long is attached to the ring, and the other end is wound around a small tack which is imbedded in the ball. When the hand is held with the fingers pointing upwards, the ball hangs out of sight behind the hand. When the hand is swung upwards and turned slightly forward, the ball will appear instantly at the finger tips.

2. THE VANISHING BALL

The magician takes a small ball from his vest pocket. He squeezes it between his hands and the ball immediately disappears.

The ball has a tack in it, and to the tack is attached a foot or more of black cord elastic, which runs through the loops of the trousers, and is tied at the further end. The ball is put in the vest pocket. When the ball is exhibited, the magician stands with his left side towards the audience, as the elastic runs under the coat from the left vest pocket. The elastic is stretched when the ball is shown, and as the hands close over the ball, it is released. Hidden by the left arm, the ball flies under the coat, and the hands are shown empty.

3. THE DIMINISHING BALL

This is a very new trick which requires a nickeled metal ball about an inch (or a little more) in diameter. The magician shows a three-inch cardboard tube, just large enough to receive the ball. The tube is painted black on the inside.

The ball is set in the tube, which is tilted slightly, and the ball slides through slowly. As people watch the ball they see it gradually diminish in size until it is about the size of a pea. Then the ball is allowed to slide back, and it emerges, its original size.

The trick is an optical illusion. The black lining of the tube throws a shadow, and makes the ball seem to diminish in size. If he wishes, the magician may have a tiny metal ball, which he holds between the fingers of his left hand at the bottom of the tube. As soon as the large ball reaches the bottom of the tube, it is caught in the bent fingers of the left hand, which carry it away, and drop the tiny ball on the table, while the right hand gives the tube for inspection.

4. THE SELF–ROLLING BALL

This is an exceptionally interesting dinner-table trick. A golf ball (or wooden ball) is laid on the table, and it mysteriously rolls across the table. While it is in motion any person may pick it up and examine it.

Method: Under the tablecloth, have a small ring, with a thread attached. The thread runs to a confederate on the other side of the table. When the ball is set on the hidden ring, and the confederate pulls the string, the ball will roll across the table. As soon as the ball is lifted, the confederate pulls the ring away from under the cloth.

The thread may be operated by the performer if he wishes. In this case it is advisable to run the thread across the table, through a screw-eye under the table and back to the magician. Thus when he pulls the thread the ball will go away from him, and not toward him, which is more effective than the simple plan of having the thread run direct to the performer.

5. THE AËRIAL BALL

A ping-pong ball is best for this trick. The ball is held in one hand, and it suddenly glides through the air to the other hand.

A loop of black thread dots the trick. The forefingers of both hands hold the loop taut, forming a sort of track along which the ball slides. The lightness of the ping-pong ball is an asset in this trick, although a light wooden ball will work.

6. BALANCED GOLF BALLS

Balancing one golf ball upon another sounds like an impossibility; and it would be, if there were not a trick to it!

3

A little dab of lead plaster, secretly attached to the upper ball, is all that is necessary. The upper ball is pressed upon the lower so that the wax comes at the contact point, and the upper ball will remain, apparently balanced.

7. THE MYSTERIOUS BALL

The magician holds a small ball in his right hand. He covers the hand with a handkerchief and turns the hand back up. He then invites several persons to reach in under the handkerchief and satisfy themselves that the ball is still in the hand. This is done, but as soon as the last person has felt the ball, the magician snatches away the cloth and the ball has disappeared!

The handkerchief is draped over the hand again and people reach under to make sure the ball has not returned. After everyone agrees that the hand is empty, the handkerchief is removed and there is the ball, back again!

This trick seems impossible, and it might be, if the magician attempted it alone. But the last person who reaches under to feel the ball is a confederate, and he calmly takes the ball away when he removes his hand! Hence the remarkable disappearance. When the empty hand is held beneath the handkerchief, the confederate reaches under—last again—and puts the ball back in the magician's hand. It is a bold trick that works.

8. THE BALL TUBE

The "Ball Tube" is an appliance that can be constructed from a cardboard mailing tube. A ball is dropped through the tube from the top, and of course it comes out at the bottom. But when the ball is dropped in again, it stops halfway, and then falls through at the magician's command. The tube is too thick to be pressed, and as the ball slides freely through, its sudden stopping and starting again is very mysterious, especially as the ball may be seen while suspended in the tube, and the tube may be so held that people can see through it.

Various means have been devised for halting the ball in its progress through the tube. The simplest device is a length of black thread stretching across the tube. One end is knotted. The other end, which is twice as long as the diameter of the tube, has a small bead tied on the end. A strip of colored paper should be pasted around the tube to hide the knotted end of the thread. The bead is covered by the thumb.

When the ball is dropped through the tube, it falls freely until the thumb draws down the bead, tightening the thread, which stops the ball. As soon as the thumb releases pressure, the ball falls again. The interior of the tube may be shown provided it is not held directly in front of the light. It is advisable to have a duplicate tube (unprepared) which may be left where some one will examine it. A light ball should be used.

9.   THE THREE PAPER BALLS

The magician rolls up three tiny balls of paper. He lays them on the table, and picking up one with the right thumb and forefinger, drops it in the left hand. He repeats with the second paper ball, and throws the third ball away. But when the left hand is opened, three paper balls roll out!

The trick is repeated, without hesitation, time after time, but with the same result; the third ball, thrown away, mysteriously emerges from the left hand.

Method: Again we employ the artifice of holding a ball concealed between the tips of the first two fingers. A fourth ball is used, and it is hidden in the right hand. The natural bend of the fingers allay suspicion. The first ball is picked up and is dropped fairly in the left hand; but when the second ball is dropped in, the hidden pellet is dropped also, the left hand immediately closing over it. When the third ball is "thrown away" it is really retained by the right finger tips. When the left hand is opened, and three balls are rolled out, the trick is ready to be repeated.

If the trick is performed seated at a dinner-table the magician should have a lump of sugar resting on his knee. After the trick has been repeated a number of times, he asks a spectator to throw away the third ball. Then his left hand rolls out three balls, and while attention is on them, the right hand picks up the lump of sugar, holding it in the bend of the fingers.

The right hand picks up two of the paper balls and drops them in the left, letting the lump fall also. Then the third ball is thrown away, and when the hand is opened, the lump of sugar rolls out instead of the third ball.

Another finish is to pick up the three balls (or two if the sugar is used) and pretend to put them in the left hand, really holding them with the right thumb and fingers. This is not difficult, as the right fingers merely slap the left palm, and the left hand closes immediately.

When the left hand is opened, the balls have vanished. The right hand, meanwhile, lets them fall over the edge of the table.

Before performing this trick, it is not a bad plan to scatter some ten or twelve paper pellets on the floor. People seeing these afterwards will think that they are paper balls which have been thrown away.

10. THE BALLS AND THE HATS

The magician rolls up four paper balls, each about the size of a golf ball. He lays them on the table so that they form the corners of a square. Then he takes two hats and puts each one over a ball. Picking up an odd ball, he reaches beneath the table, and thumps the bottom of the table. A hat is lifted, and there is the second ball! The hat is replaced over the two balls; the other odd ball is thumped under the table, and three balls appear beneath the hat. The three balls are covered with the hat, and the magician points to the other hat, which has a ball beneath it. He lifts the hat, and shows it empty. The ball has gone! And when the three-ball hat is lifted, all four balls are beneath it!

The trick usually ends here, but there is a very surprising conclusion which may be introduced. The empty hat is laid on the table. The four balls are set upon it, and the other hat is pressed down on top. When both hats are lifted they reveal a large paper ball, as big as the hat itself!

The first part of the trick is not difficult of execution. When the magician starts to place one hat over each of two balls, he is uncertain which of the paper balls to cover. He puts the right hand over the ball nearest him; and his fingers, which are underneath the hat, grip the ball, while the other hand is deciding where to put its hat. Suddenly he lifts the right-hand hat, carrying the ball beneath it, and instantly drops the left-hand hat upon the space occupied by the right-hand hat. As the hats come together, no one has a chance to see that the ball is no longer there. The right hand drops the hat (and the ball) over another ball.

The right hand then picks up an odd ball and thumps it beneath the table. The left hand picks up the hat and reveals two paper balls. The left hand carries the hat to the edge of the table, where it is gripped by the right hand. The fingers of the right hand go inside the hat, holding the ball there. The hat is dropped over the two balls and the third ball drops with it.

This maneuver is repeated with the other odd ball, so that three balls appear beneath the hat; and then the fourth ball is secretly introduced. When the magician points to the other hat which is supposed to cover a ball, he has merely to lift the hat, show it empty, and then let someone lift the other hat and find all four balls!

If the magician adds the large ball effect, he goes about it thus: The large ball is hidden under the coat, on the left side of the body. It rests against the magician's hip.

The magician shows the one hat empty, picking it up with his right hand. Then he transfers it to the left hand, which holds the mouth of the hat close against the body. A person is requested to lift the other hat. As this is done, all eyes will be upon the four balls which appear beneath it. No one will be looking at the magician. As he leans forward and gazes at the four balls on the table, his right hand reaches beneath the coat and slides the large ball into the hat held by the left hand. Then both hands immediately drop the hat crown upward on the table. Everything is then set for the mysterious appearance of the large paper ball.

11. THE FLOATING PAPER BALL

The "Floating Paper Ball" is a very pretty little experiment, when performed under proper conditions.

The magician crumples a piece of paper into a ball, and holds it in his left hand, with his right hand above it. He takes his left hand away, and the ball floats in the air, rising slowly to the right hand.

The trick is accomplished with a piece of black silk thread. A loop is formed in one end, and is placed over the magician's right ear. The other end is attached loosely to a coat button.

When the paper ball is formed, it is squeezed around the loose end of the thread. When the right hand goes above the ball, it catches the thread over the right thumb, and draws the thread taut, so that when the left hand is removed, the ball floats. Advancing the hand raises the ball, withdrawing it lowers the ball.

Finally the left hand takes the ball and draws it from the thread. The right hand brushes back the hair, and in so doing lifts the loop from the ear, letting the thread fall to the floor.

12. RED, WHITE AND BLUE

The magician makes nine paper balls from tissue paper—three red, three white and three blue.

He also uses three hats. He puts a red ball in the first hat, a white in the second and a blue in the third. He repeats this, so that one hat contains three red balls, another three white, and the third three blue.

But when the hats are turned over, each one is seen to contain a red, a white, and a blue ball!

A bit of easy manipulation is necessary here. The hats will be termed 1, 2, and 3.

A red ball is apparently dropped in hat 1, but it is scooped up and held concealed in the fingers of the hand.

A white ball is apparently dropped into 2; but it is retained, and the red is dropped in. A blue is picked up, and secretly retained, while the white falls in 3.

A red ball is apparently dropped in 1, but is retained and the blue drops in. A blue is apparently dropped in 3, but the red goes in. A white apparently goes in 2, but the blue is really dropped in.

A red is dropped into 1, and the white is let fall with it. A white is dropped in 2, and a blue is dropped in 3.

These movements are not difficult to perform as the balls are small. The trick should be practiced with the paper balls, and it will prove very easy to follow.

13. MULTIPLYING PAPER BALLS

This is an impromptu form of the "Multiplying Ball" trick which is very effective when properly presented.

The magician rolls a piece of paper into a tight ball, and squeezes it very compactly. He holds it between the tips of his thumb and forefinger, and suddenly it doubles, another ball appearing between his first and second finger.

He throws the balls on the table; picks them up, and puts one between his thumb and forefinger and the other between his second and third fingers. This time another ball appears between them.

There are three paper balls at the outset. Two are already prepared and are held concealed in the left hand, while the other ball is formed in plain view. One of the hidden balls is added to it, and the two are held as one. By simply lifting up with the second finger, the second ball is made to appear beside the first. The balls are thrown on the table, and one is picked up with each hand. While the right hand adjusts its ball between the second and third fingers, the left hand adds the hidden ball to the first one, and the two are put between the thumb and forefinger of the right hand. A lift up with the right second finger, and the third ball comes into view.

14. THE THREE MARBLE TRICK

The magician shows three marbles in one hand. He tosses them back and forth between his hands, showing three each time. He finally holds them in his left hand, and asks a person to say how many are there. Of course the answer is "three," but when the hand is opened, *four* marbles are seen.

At the beginning, there are three marbles in the right hand, and one of them rests at the base of the two middle fingers. An extra marble is similarly held in the left hand.

When the magician tosses three marbles into the left hand, he really tosses two, retaining the one. But he immediately opens the left hand and shows three there. The marbles are tossed back and forth several times, and always three may be shown, the fourth being retained. This movement is absolutely deceptive.

On the last toss the extra right hand marble goes into the left, so the left has four marbles when it is opened.

CHAPTER II

CARD TRICKS

Card tricks constitute the broadest field of impromptu magic. There are many magicians who specialize in card tricks only, and the skillful sleights and passes that are possible with cards are exceedingly numerous. On the other hand, there are many perplexing tricks with cards that require very little skill, and some of the best of these form the present chapter.

Before attempting to perform card tricks, the amateur magician should first learn to shuffle and deal cards with ease and precision. If he handles the pack clumsily, the people watching him will quickly realize that he is not performing feats of skill; but if he proceeds with smoothness, they will attribute his tricks to skill in sleight-of-hand, and will take an interest in his performing.

A great many card tricks consist of the surprising discovery or revelation of a certain card which has apparently been chosen at random by a spectator. Therefore, the magician must find ways of learning, or of controlling a selected card, either before or after it is taken from the pack. We will first consider a number of simple but effective methods by which this end may be accomplished. There are other methods which form intrinsic parts of certain tricks, and they will be explained later in the chapter.

1. THE "ONE–WAY" PACK

Certain packs of cards have what is known as "one-way" backs. This is particularly true of high-grade cards. Instead of a symmetrical design on the backs of the cards, these packs have pictures or initials. Such a pack is especially suited to the needs of the magician. He first arranges the cards so that the pictures are all pointed in the same direction. Then he fans the cards and allows a person to select one. As soon as the card has been drawn, the magician quietly turns the pack around. Thus when the chosen card is returned, its design will be reversed. The pack may be shuffled, but as soon as the magician runs through the cards, he will discover the one that is reversed, and will know that it is the chosen card.

"Bicycle" cards do not, as a rule, have "one-way" backs. There is one exception, however, in the pattern known as the "Emblem Back." This design is reversible, although it does not appear so at first glance. Such a pack is the best available for this trick.

2. THE PENCIL–MARK PACK

Any pack of cards may be made "one-way" by a very simple process. Square up the pack and make two or three straight pencil lines at one end of the pack, the lines crossing every card. When a card is selected, the pack is turned around, and the chosen card is returned. A glance at the marked end of the pack will reveal a break in the pencil lines; at the other end of the pack, tiny pencil dots will appear. The breaks at one end and the dots at the other indicate the chosen card, and the pack should be cut at that point.

3. POINTED CARDS

A glance through a pack of cards will reveal the fact that certain cards are "pointers." Take for example, the seven of spades. It has seven spots and five of them point in one direction. The nine of hearts has five points in one direction. The aces of spades, hearts, and clubs are "pointers." The seven of diamonds is a "pointer," because it has one odd point above the center.

CARD TRICKS

To make use of this interesting principle, take all the "pointers" from a pack, and arrange them with their principal points in one direction. Group these cards at the center of the pack, and fan the cards so that one of the "pointers" will be selected. Turn the pack around, and let the chosen card be returned. After the pack has been shuffled, a glance at the faces of the cards will reveal the chosen card, for it will be pointing the opposite way from the others.

4. THE DOUBLE CARD

This is an ideal form of "card locator" for the magician who performs with his own pack. A pack of cards with white margins should be used. Take the odd card which generally comes with such packs and trim off the white margin. Then paste the trimmed card on the back of one of the cards in the pack. At a very close distance, the double thickness cannot be detected.

As soon as a card has been taken from the pack, square up the cards and riffle one end of the pack. Your finger will encounter a sudden stop as soon as the double card falls. Let the chosen card be replaced at that point, and it will be directly above the double card. Then the pack may be squared up and cut. Your fingers will naturally lift off the cards above the double card, and thus the chosen card will be brought to the bottom of the pack.

5. THE SHORT CARD

The short card serves the same purpose as the double card. It is simply a card which has about a sixteenth of an inch trimmed from one end. It is handled just the same as the double card and serves as a locator when the chosen card is replaced just above it.

The short card, however, may be adapted to any pack of cards, if the magician takes the precaution to carry a pair of small scissors (preferably folding ones) in his pocket. By pocketing a card from the pack, and finding an opportunity to leave the room, he may trim the end of the card and return it to the borrowed pack.

6. THE BENT CORNER

In this trick, the magician fans the pack and holds the cards with the faces toward a spectator, inviting him to touch one of the cards. As soon as the spectator does so, the magician's left thumb, which is hidden behind the pack, bends up the corner of the selected card. After the pack has been shuffled, a glance at the corner of the pack reveals the position of the chosen card, and the pack can be cut at that point.

7. FALSE SHUFFLING

False shuffling is the means whereby a card may be kept at the top or the bottom of the pack while the magician is shuffling the cards. A false shuffle should not be shown as a trick in itself. No especial skill is required in false shuffles; anyone who can shuffle a pack of cards in the ordinary manner can execute the false shuffle just as easily.

First, suppose that the pack is to be shuffled in the dovetail fashion, by cutting it into two heaps and riffling the ends together. The magician has located the chosen card and has cut the cards to bring it to the top of the pack. In riffling the ends of the pack, he merely retains the top card with his thumb, so that it is the last card to fall and its position is undisturbed.

Second, for an ordinary shuffle, to keep the chosen card on top of the pack, grip the pack between the thumb and fingers of the right hand, the thumb at one end and the fingers at the other. Hold the pack with the bottom card facing the audience. Now the left thumb comes up, and pulls away some of the cards from the bottom of the pack. As it does so, the left fingers bring along the top card also. Then the right hand, aided by the left thumb, shuffles the remaining cards in front of the first group. The chosen card still remains on top. If the chosen card is originally on the bottom, the right hand holds the pack with the back of the top card toward the audience. Otherwise the shuffle is the same.*

Third, there is a very simple shuffle in which the chosen card is undetectably transferred from the top of the pack to the bottom, or vice versa. Hold the pack as previously described, with the top card toward the audience. The left thumb pulls away the top card alone and the remaining cards are then shuffled on top of it, so that the chosen card becomes the bottom card. To bring the bottom card to the top, the magician should first take the precaution of turning his right side toward the audience; then he takes the pack between the fingers and thumb of his right hand, with the top card toward the palm. The left thumb pulls down the bottom card alone, letting it fall into the bend of the left fingers; then the remaining cards are shuffled from the right hand into the left, the desired card then being on top of the pack.

8. CUT TO THE CARD

The items previously described in this chapter are not complete card tricks in themselves. They are methods that lead up to clever conclusions which would be impossible without their aid. The following trick, which is a great mystery, is dependent upon a method given before.

Effect: A card is chosen and returned to the pack, which is thoroughly shuffled. The magician takes a card from the pack, and exhibits it. It is not the chosen card. With a sudden movement, he thrusts the card face up into the center of the pack, and using it as a lever, lifts off the upper portion of the pack. When

---

* In order to avoid confusion, the reader should study all card tricks with the pack in his hands. He should begin by laying the cards on the table as though ready to be dealt. The uppermost card is then known as the TOP card; the lowermost is the BOTTOM card. These conditions are *always* considered the same, no matter in what position the pack may be held.

he turns the upper portion face up, behold! the chosen card is on the bottom of the upper portion! The quick thrust into the pack has discovered the chosen card.

Method: Refer to trick 6 of the present chapter. The trick is performed by the aid of the bent corner. When the magician holds the pack, he turns the edge toward himself and looks for the bent corner, which stands out quite plainly. It is a simple matter to thrust the odd card, face up, just below the card with the bent corner.

9. THE SPELLING TRICK

A card is selected from the pack and is reinserted. The magician cuts the pack several times. Then he asks the name of the chosen card. Suppose it is the queen of clubs. He deals off the cards one by one, spelling a letter as he deals each card, thus: "Q-U-E-E-N O-F C-L-U-B-S." He turns up the last card. It is the queen of clubs!

Method: After a card has been taken from the pack, square up the cards in the left hand and then start to push the top cards to the side so that the chosen card may be inserted. In so doing, count the cards as your left thumb pushes them to the right, and as soon as you have reached eleven, calmly lift that group of cards, and let the chosen card be placed under them. This must be done nonchalantly. After your right hand has lifted the eleven cards, the left thumb should still push along a few more cards in a careless manner, but the break should be made just below the eleventh card.

The selected card is then the twelfth from the top of the pack. Cut the pack into four heaps, and lay them thus:

1   2   3   4

Heap 4 is the top heap, and it should contain at least fifteen cards. Throw heap 4 on heap 2. Then drop heap 3 on heap 1, and place heaps 2 and 4 on 1 and 3. This apparently mixes the cards, but it does not change the position of the top twelve.*

Then ask the name of the chosen card. *No matter what that card may be, you can spell its name in such a way that your count will end on the twelfth card.*

For example, ace of spades: Spell A-C-E O-F S-P-A-D-E-S, and turn up the *next* card.

Ace of clubs: Turn the top card of the pack face up and appear surprised to find that it is not the ace of clubs. Toss it aside, and start spelling with the second card: A-C-E O-F C-L-U-B-S, and turn up the *next* card.

Ace of diamonds: Spell A-C-E O-F D-I-A-M-O-N-D. Turn up the last card on the letter D. It will be the ace of diamonds.

Queen of diamonds: Spell Q-U-E-E-N D-I-A-M-O-N-D and turn up the card on letter D.

King of diamonds: Spell K-I-N-G D-I-A-M-O-N-D-S and turn up the card on the letter S.

By employing one of these various methods to suit the chosen card you can always end your spelling on the twelfth card. The joker should not be used in the pack. As soon as the chosen card is named, you can do the spelling mentally, or with your finger tips. With a little practice the trick presents no difficulties.

10. THE WISE QUEEN

This is a very effective mystery. A spectator is invited to shuffle the pack. The magician takes the cards and asks, "Which is your favorite queen?" Suppose the queen of diamonds is named. The magician runs through the pack and removes the queen of diamonds. Then he lays the pack face down on the table and divides it into three piles. The spectator selects one of the piles and

---

* This procedure is known as a "False Cut." It may be employed in other tricks instead of using a "false shuffle."

removes the top card; he lays it face down on the table without looking at it.

The magician remarks that the queen of diamonds is very wise. He holds the queen to his ear, and pretends to converse with it. Then he touches the queen to the card that is on the table, and again holds the queen to his ear.

"Ah!" he says, "The queen tells me that that card is the nine of spades." The card is turned up, and it *is* the nine of spades!

Method: In looking through the pack to find the queen of diamonds, the magician calmly glimpses the top card and remembers it. When he cuts the pack, he lifts off about two-thirds, leaving a small heap; then he moves to the right and drops another third; and he drops the top group in the center. He therefore knows the top card of the center heap, which we are assuming to be the nine of spades. When the magician asks a spectator directly in front of him to choose a heap, that person will almost invariably take the center heap, which fits right in with the magician's plans. The top card of the heap is chosen, and the rest of the trick is merely by-play.

Should the spectator choose another heap, the magician need not worry, for he has not yet stated what he intends to do. He turns to another person and says, "You take one also," at the same time indicating the other end heap with a wave of his hand. If the spectator takes that heap, the magician says, "Now we have one heap left. We will use it."

If the second spectator takes the center heap, the magician immediately forgets the first person, and centering his attention on the second person, tells him to lay aside the top card of his heap.

11. FINDING A CHOSEN CARD

A pack of cards is divided into two portions. A spectator selects a card from one half, and places it in the other, which is shuffled.

The magician looks through the half of the pack and immediately discovers the chosen card!

Method: In one half of the pack are all the *odd* cards—ace, three, five, seven, nine, jack, and king. The other half contains the *even* cards. No one will notice this.

When a card is placed from one section to the other, the magician can immediately discover it when he looks through that portion of the pack.

12.   THE X-RAY CARD CASE

The magician takes a pack of cards from the case. He holds the case behind his back and invites anyone to insert a card, face down, in the case, closing the flap of the case so that the card will be entirely concealed.

The magician then holds the cardcase to his forehead and instantly names the card that is in the case, although no one has seen it!

Method: A small hole is cut in the lower right corner of the back of the card case. The case is held back downwards, behind the back, with the thumb always covering the tiny opening.

In raising the case to his forehead, the magician moves his thumb aside and thus catches a glimpse of the index corner of the card inside the case.

13.   THE COLOR-CHANGING PACK

Effect: The magician exhibits a pack of cards with the joker on the face (the bottom). He riffles the end of the pack, and shows that it contains red cards only. He blows on the pack, and riffles it again. This time the cards are all black! He blows on the pack once more, and this time the cards become both red and black. The pack may be thoroughly examined.

Method: Separate the reds from the black, and dovetail the two portions very carefully, so that every odd card is red, and every even card black. Push the two sections together, but stop before the ends are quite flush. Then put the joker on the bottom of the

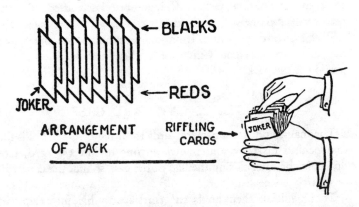

JOKER ← BLACKS

← REDS

ARRANGEMENT OF PACK

RIFFLING CARDS →

JOKER

pack. The result is this: When one end of the pack is riffled, only red cards will be seen. In blowing on the cards, and transferring them from one hand to the other, they are turned around, and when the other end is riffled, only blacks will appear. In blowing on the cards again, the fingers push the two sections flush together; so when the cards are riffled the third time, both colors will be in evidence.

The pack must be held quite firmly during the trick.

14. THE COLOR–CHANGING CARD

This is a very smart and surprising trick. The magician turns the top card of the pack face up and shows that it is the six of diamonds. He throws the pack upon the floor, and the card instantly changes into the six of spades.

Method: The second card of the pack is the six of spades. Just before dropping the pack, push the two top cards, as though they were one, about three-quarters of an inch over the side of the pack. The pack must be thrown squarely upon the floor, and not too violently, or the cards will scatter. The pressure of the air causes the two top cards to turn over, so that the six of diamonds falls face down, while the six of spades comes face up. To the observer, it appears as though the six of diamonds has magically been transformed into the six of spades in the twinkling of an eye.

15. THE THREE JACKS

The majority of tricks do not bear repetition, but here is one that becomes more and more perplexing as it is repeated. It should not be overdone, however.

The magician takes the pack and deals two heaps of three cards each, dealing the cards one at a time. He turns up the first hand dealt and shows that it contains three jacks. He gathers up the cards and repeats the deal; again the first hand receives the three jacks. The deal is repeated several times, yet every time the three jacks fall in the first hand.

This is apparently a feat of skillful dealing, but in reality, no dexterity is required. *Four* jacks actually figure in the trick. On the top of the pack are three jacks, then an indifferent card, and then the fourth jack. The cards are dealt one at a time, in two heaps of three each; but when the sixth card is dealt, it must be slid under the second heap, being used as a lever to pick up that heap and put it back on the pack. Then the first heap is shown to contain three jacks, which are replaced on the pack. The cards are then set to repeat the trick.

16. CARD AT ANY NUMBER

Effect: After a card has been selected and returned to the pack, the magician states that he will make that card appear any number down from the top of the pack. Suppose that the number sixteen is requested. He counts off sixteen cards, and turns up the last one, but it is not the chosen card. Rather surprised at this, the magician hands the pack to the chooser and tells him to count the number for himself. When the spectator counts off sixteen cards, he finds that his card is the sixteenth.

Method: The selected card is brought to the top of the pack by one of the methods previously explained; and is kept there by a "false shuffle." When a person calls for sixteen, the magician counts off sixteen cards one by one, and replaces them on the pack, before he turns up the last removed. Of course it is not the chosen card; but in counting the cards the magician has reversed their order so that the sixteenth card now is the chosen one, ready for the person to count to it.

17. THE CARD IN THE POCKET

This trick depends upon a variation of the principle just explained. A pack of cards is shuffled, and the magician tells a person to count off any number of cards, say ten, and then look at the next card (the eleventh) after which he is to replace the cards he has counted off, leaving the selected card in its original position.

This is done while the magician's back is turned. Then the pack is given to him and, looking through the cards, he removes one and puts it in his pocket. The pack is given back to the spectator, who is told to count down to his card; but when he reaches the eleventh card, he finds that his card is gone. The magician thereupon removes the chosen card from his pocket! It must be remembered that the magician *does not know* the number of cards counted off by the spectator, and this makes the trick appear very mysterious.

Method: In giving the pack to the spectator and explaining how he must count off the cards, the magician notes the top card. In counting the cards off one by one, the spectator reverses the order of the cards. When he looks at the eleventh card and puts the ten cards back on top, the *card which the magician knows* comes directly over the chosen card. The magician merely has to look for his own card and remove the card below it.

18. THE TURN–UP CARD

The Turn-Up Card is a very pretty conclusion for a card trick. The magician simply slides the pack along the table, and the chosen card mysteriously turns over in the middle of the pack, and lies face up.

In its original form, this trick was done by having the chosen card on top of the pack, brought there by the magician's customary method. As the pack was dropped, the top card was allowed to project, as in the Color-Changing Card, so that it would turn face up on the pack.

In the improved method, the magician holds the pack crosswise in his right hand. The right thumb pushes forward the top card and the fingers lift it slightly. Then he slides the cards along the table, in an easy sweep. The air pressure turns over the top card, which falls in the midst of the sliding cards just as though it emerged from the center of the pack.

There is nothing difficult about this trick, but there is a certain easy knack that, once acquired, makes the trick a perfect illusion.

19. THE BURGLARS

There is an old trick called the "Four Burglars," which is now so ancient that it is hardly worth performing. There is, however, a new adaptation of the trick which is entirely different in method, and it makes a very interesting experiment in impromptu magic.

Three jacks are shown, representing three burglars. A king is also used to represent a detective, while the pack represents a house.

The story goes as follows: "The three burglars decided to rob the house, so one went in the front door." (A jack is placed on the bottom of the pack.) "Another entered the back door." (A jack goes on top.) "The third went in a window." (The third jack is pushed into the center of the pack.) "The detective seeing this, went in the back door also." (The king is placed on top.)

"The burglars, hearing the detective, ran around in the house." (Here the pack is cut three times.)

The pack is then fanned, and in the center of the pack are found the three burglars, each one guarded by two detectives. That is, in the center of the pack, seven cards are discovered clustered together in the following order: King, jack, king, jack, king, jack, king.

Before commencing the trick, secretly place the fourth jack between two kings at the bottom of the pack, and put a king on top of the pack. No one knows of this preparation. When one jack "goes in the window," push it in the pack quite a little above the center. Place the other cards as described. Then when you cut the cards, the three jacks and four kings will be together as described. One cut is sufficient, but two additional cuts add to the effect.

20. KINGS AND QUEENS

Effect: The four kings and four queens are removed from the pack. They are gathered together in a pile, which is cut and apparently thoroughly mixed. The magician puts the cards behind his back and brings out the king and queen of clubs, then the king and queen of spades, then diamonds, and finally hearts. All the kings and queens are paired!

The cards are stacked together again, and the heap is cut. This time the magician brings out the four kings in one hand and the four queens in the other.

Method: In arranging the cards, lay the four queens together,

24

and the four kings together; take care that the order of suits is the same in each group; say diamonds, clubs, spades, hearts. Put the two groups together. The packet may be cut any number of times, and you can make this more effective by taking off three or four cards from the top and putting them on the bottom, and then peeling off five or six cards from the bottom and placing them on the top, all in one continued movement.

Simply put the cards behind your back and hold them in your left hand, your forefinger separating the top four cards from the lower so that you have two packets. With your right hand take the top cards from each group. They will be the king and queen of the same suit. The next two cards will also be of the same suit and so on.

For the second part of the trick, put the paired kings and queens in one group, but take care that their order runs king, queen, king, queen, king, queen, king, queen; or queen, king, queen, etc. Put the cards behind your back and draw off the top card between the right thumb and forefinger; the second between the forefinger and second finger. Proceed thus so that the odd cards are in one group, the evens in the other. One group will contain the kings, the other the queens.

21. MENTAL TELEPATHY

The magician shows three cards and asks a person to think of one of them. He puts the three cards in his trousers pocket. Then he draws out two of the cards and lays them on the pack.

"If you have been thinking of your card," announces the magician, "it will be the one that is still in my pocket. Tell everyone the name of your card."

"The three of clubs," replies the person who is thinking of the card.

The magician reaches in his pocket and brings out the three of clubs.

In his pocket, the magician has previously hidden two in-different cards. When he shows three cards, and puts them in his pocket, he notices the order in which they lie. Then he reaches in and brings out the two indifferent cards, but does not show their faces. The audience believes that they are two of the three cards he just put in his pocket.

When the spectator names the card of which he is thinking, the magician has simply to bring out the correct one of the three cards that are in his pocket!

He then has two cards remaining, so he can repeat the trick. By watching a person's eyes, it is often possible to discover the card he is choosing, in which case the secreted cards do not have to be used; instead, the magician can bring out the two cards that the person is *not* thinking of, and carelessly drop them face up. This diverts suspicion from the usual method.

22. LONG DISTANCE TELEPATHY

This is an excellent trick to perform in connection with the previous experiment. After your audience is worked up to the height of perplexity, ask them to choose any card from the entire pack. Suppose the ace of hearts is selected. You then state that if all present will concentrate on the ace of hearts, any person may call up your friend Mr. Adams, whose telephone number is Market 1416 (or whatever the number may be), and he will name the card selected.

This is done, and when Mr. Adams comes to the other end of the wire, he promptly names the ace of hearts as the card selected.

This trick will never fail to create astonishment: but the secret is very simple. On a card in your pocket, you have a list of names, such as the list on page 27.

When you look on the card for the phone number of your friend, you also find the name that goes with the playing card that has been selected by the company. If the eight of spades is

CARD TRICKS

selected, you tell the audience to call up and ask for **Mr. Hood.**
Mr. Klein is the key name for the jack of clubs, and so on.

	Diamonds	Clubs	Hearts	Spades
Ace	Alberts	Ames	Adams	Atkinson
Two	Brown	Bates	Billings	Black
Three	Carter	Chester	Crown	Callahan
Four	Davis	Dodd	Dale	Dobbins
Five	Earle	Emerson	Ellis	Engle
Six	Franks	Fisher	Farnum	Flood
Seven	Graham	Gibson	Girard	Glover
Eight	Harris	Hale	Herbert	Hood
Nine	Irwin	Idler	Ives	Ingersoll
Ten	James	Judson	Jansen	Jarvis
Jack	Knight	Klein	Kaufman	Keyser
Queen	Lewis	Lane	Lawrence	Lee
King	Morris	Moore	Myers	Mulholland

Joker—Rice

Your friend at the other end of the line has a duplicate list, so as
soon as the fictitious name is given to him he knows the chosen
card. Note the alphabetical arrangement of the list.

The trick cannot be repeated. Your excuse for this is that so
much concentration is necessary that your "mind reader" can
only visualize one card in the course of an evening; so if the trick
were repeated, he would simply repeat the name of the first card
chosen.

23. MAGNETIC CARDS

The effect of the Magnetic Card trick is quite surprising. The
magician lays a number of cards on the palm of his hand, and
when he turns the hand over, the cards remain attached to it, as

though magnetized; until, at the magician's command, they fall to the floor.

There are several methods of working this trick, and an explanation of different ways of performing will enable the reader to use the method which best suits him.

Method 1: Tie a fine hair around the center of the hand, so that it forms a loop about the palm. Tuck one card under the hair, and push the other cards—seven or eight of them—under the corners of the first card. The first card will then support the others. The hair is invisible at a short distance; and a spreading of the hand will break it, releasing the cards at the desired moment.

Method 2: Use a pack of cards with an ornamental circle in the center of the back design. Cut one of the circles out of an odd card, bend the circle in half, and paste it to the center of another card so that it forms a flap. The flap is gripped between the fingers, which thus support the card, while other cards may be tucked under the supporting card. When the fingers are spread slightly, the cards will fall.

Method 3: Bend up one corner of a card and grip that corner between the last two fingers, so that the card runs diagonally across the palm. Pressure by the base of the thumb, at the other end of the card holds the card in place, so that other cards may be tucked into place.

Method 4: If you customarily wear a finger ring, insert the point of a pin under the ring, and tuck a card under the head of the pin, which extends towards the palm. This will support that card, and the other cards may be tucked in under it.*

Method 5: Obtain a piece of diachylon (lead plaster) from a drug store, and rub it all over the palm and fingers. The appearance of the hand will not be changed, but the hand will be very sticky. Lay six or seven cards on the table, and press the hand

---

* In tucking cards in under the supporting card, other cards may be inserted under the *secondary cards,* so that they will partly mask the face of the supporting card.

firmly upon them. Then lift, and the cards will come up. When the hand is shaken the cards will fall.

24. THE VANISHING CARD

This trick is performed with a playing card, a tumbler, and a handkerchief. The card is placed beneath the handkerchief, which is held over the glass; and the card is pushed down into the glass. When the handkerchief is removed, the glass is shown empty. The playing card is really a piece of transparent celluloid, cut to the size and shape of a playing card. The celluloid card is hidden beneath the handkerchief, at the outset. When an ordinary card is shown and placed beneath the handkerchief, it is dropped on the table among the remaining cards of the pack, and the celluloid card is held underneath the handkerchief, where it appears and feels like an ordinary card. When the celluloid card goes in the glass, the handkerchief may be removed and the glass held up for all to see; for the celluloid will be invisible through the sides of the glass.

25. THE AUTOMATIC RISING CARD

A drinking-glass is employed in this trick also. Any card is taken from the pack and is pushed down into the glass. A spectator is told to ask the card to rise. The card, however, does not obey the command. The magician removes the card from the glass, strokes it on his sleeve, and inserts it in the glass, from which it immediately rises to his outstretched hand.

Method: Use a smooth-finished glazed card, and a glass with tapering sides. Take a piece of dry soap and rub it on the inside of the glass, making two narrow channels at opposite points, running from the top of the glass to the bottom. When the card is pushed down into the glass so that its edges come in contact with the smooth paths, the card will rise; but if it is not pushed in at the correct point, it will not rise. The soap should be applied carefully and evenly; then its presence will not be observable.

26. THE CARD ON THE HAND

This is a surprising finish to a card trick. After a chosen card has been brought on top of the pack by any one of the methods described, the pack is cut into two portions. The magician places the lower portion on the palm of his hand and tosses it in the air. He thrusts his hand among the falling cards, and the chosen card appears on the back of his hand, apparently caught out of the others.

Method: The magician has a tiny bit of lead plaster affixed to the back of his hand. When he places the lower heap on the palm of the hand, he momentarily rests the back of the hand on the upper heap. When the hand tosses the lower heap in the air, the chosen card sticks to the back of the hand. The hand is simply turned over amongst the falling cards, and the illusion is complete.

27. THE SPIRIT CARD

The Spirit Card is a perfect little mystery that requires a mimimum of skill. An envelope is shown empty, and a tiny piece of cardboard is put in it. Then a pack of cards is cut and the envelope is inserted between the two halves of the pack. The spectators then look at the card just below the envelope. It is the four of diamonds. The envelope is opened, and the tiny card is shaken out. On it is a picture of the four of diamonds! The envelope is then tossed on the table.

Method: The envelope is a double one, made by cutting off the front of another envelope and inserting it in a genuine envelope. When the two flaps are stuck together, the envelope appears quite innocent.*

* It is best to use a small envelope with the flap at the end.

In the front compartment of the envelope, place the tiny four of diamonds (or whatever card you wish to use). The tiny card can be drawn with ink; a tiny photograph or a printed card is preferable if one can be obtained.

The top card of the pack is a four of diamonds. Show the envelope apparently empty, and drop in a blank card of the same size as the miniature that is hidden in the envelope. Cut the pack, and after sealing the envelope, calmly place it on the top portion of the pack, putting the lower portion on the envelope. This is a bold procedure that never fails to pass detection. The spectators look at the card underneath the envelope.

Remove the envelope, cut it under the flap, thus opening the front compartment, and let the tiny card fall out. While every one is examining it, and the surprise is great, calmly put the envelope in your pocket. There you have a duplicate envelope, which is unprepared, and which has been sealed and opened. As an afterthought, you bring out the envelope (really the duplicate) and drop it carelessly on the table. No one ever notices this simple exchange, as it is done quite naturally. Do not say anything about the envelope; after a while some one will pick it up and examine it.

28. THE ACES FROM THE POCKET

Allow a pack of cards to be thoroughly shuffled. Show that the inside pocket of your coat is quite empty, and put the pack in there. State that the aces respond to your sense of touch, and thrust your hand into the pocket. Each time you reach in, you bring out an ace! After the aces have all been produced, the pack is brought out, and all the cards may be examined.

Method: Previously remove the aces from the pack, and put them in your upper right vest pocket. Let the pack be shuffled; no one will notice that the aces are missing, as you do not mention them until you have put the pack in your inside pocket.

Each time you reach for an ace, put your hand in your *vest* pocket. By holding the coat well over with the right hand, no one can tell that you are not reaching into the inside pocket.

29. THE REVERSING CARD

The effect of this trick is not new; but the method has been so simplified that the trick may be performed with very little practice.

A card is taken from the pack and noted. It is returned to the magician, who pushes it face down into the pack, holding the pack well squared to show that he cannot keep track of the card.

The pack is laid on the table and the magician waves his hand over it. He deals off the cards one by one, and suddenly he comes to a card that is face up. It is the chosen card!

To perform this trick, use a pack that has white margins around the edges of the backs. Secretly turn the bottom card of the pack face up. Then fan the cards, taking care not to show the bottom card, and have a card selected.

While those present are looking at the card, turn your back so that you will not see it. This gives you time to square up the pack and turn it over, so that the bottom card is on top.* When you put the chosen card back in the center of the pack, it really goes in upside down; the reversed bottom card makes the pack appear normal. Hold the pack in your left hand, the fingers at one side and the thumb at the other, with the palm upwards. As you approach the table, turn your hand over (back up) with a sweeping motion, and lay the pack on the table. Pass your hand over the pack and deal the cards until you come to the chosen card, which will be face up.

* The reversal of the bottom card may be left until you turn your back, but it is safer to attend to it beforehand if possible.

30. THE TRAVELING ACE

Take a pack of cards and show the ace of clubs, which you place on top of the pack for a moment. Then remove the card and push it into the center of the pack; when the card is one-third in, tilt the pack up so that everyone may glimpse the ace.

As soon as the ace is fairly in the pack, the cards are snapped, and the bottom card is turned up. It is the ace of clubs, back on top!

Method: When you show the ace of clubs, the three of clubs is in back of it, the two being held as one. The cards should be bent slightly outwards by pressure of the thumb and fingers at opposite sides. Then the double thickness will not be detected. The cards are laid on the pack, and the three (supposedly the ace) is removed and pushed in the center. When the card is one-third in, tilt up the pack, holding your finger tips over the end of the card. Only the center spot of the trey will be observed; push the card all the way in, and everyone will be satisfied that the ace is actually in the center of the pack.

31. MALTESE CROSSES

The magician states that he will play a joke on his audience. He arranges eight cards in two groups so that they form two Maltese crosses. Then he invites a person to choose any four of the cards—one cross or the other; or four cards in a line—or any combination that pleases him. This is done and the four cards are removed.

From the four remaining cards, two are selected; and finally of the two that remain, one is chosen. The final card is turned up, and it proves to be the joker!

This is artfully accomplished. The magician knows the position of the joker among the eight cards that are laid face down. If the joker is in the four cards first chosen, the magician removes the other four cards. If it is *not* in the first four, the magician *picks up* the four that are chosen.

He repeats this procedure with the four cards that remain, either leaving or picking up the two that are chosen. When the final choice is made, the magician picks up the card if it is *not* the joker; but if it is the joker, he removes the extra card, leaving the joker on the table.

When this trick is performed in a nonchalant manner, its effect is very mystifying.

32. A MYSTERIOUS COINCIDENCE

The magician asks that a pack of cards be shuffled. He takes it and shuffles it a little himself. Then he lays the pack on the table, and writes something on a piece of paper which he gives to a person to hold.

Another person now deals off any number of cards—say eight—one by one, immediately replacing them on the pack.

Then the first person deals off the same number of cards, and turns up the last one. He is told to look at his slip of paper, and it bears the name of the card he has turned up!

After the magician takes the pack to shuffle it, he secretly notes the top card of the pack. Or better, he notes the bottom card, and in shuffling, draws off all the pack from the bottom card and shuffles the cards beneath it, thus bringing the bottom card to the top.

That is the card whose name he writes on the slip of paper.

When another person deals off some cards one by one, he *reverses their order* as he lays them faces down on the table. Thus if he deals *eight* cards, the card the magician has written becomes the *eighth card from the top*. So when the first spectator deals off the same number of cards, he naturally comes to the card that corresponds to the written message.

33. A CARD THROUGH THE PLATE

A card is chosen and replaced in the pack. The magician shuffles and cuts the cards. He lays them on the table and exhibits a plate and a hat.

He lays the pack of cards on the plate, which is set upon the hat. Then he says "Pass", and when the pack is examined, the chosen card is gone. The plate is lifted and the card is found in the hat!

When the chosen card is returned to the pack, the magician tilts up the faces of the cards so that the chooser can have a last look at his card. This gives the magician an opportunity to bend up the inner corner of the chosen card with his thumb, as the pack is held fanned, and the chosen card is not entirely in.

He then shuffles the pack, and when he cuts it, he cuts at the spot in the pack where he sees the bent corner forming a hump. This brings the chosen card to the top of the pack.

There is a dab of soap on the bottom of the plate. After showing the plate the magician shows the hat, and carelessly lets the plate rest on the pack. Thus the plate picks up the chosen card.

In setting the plate on the hat, the chosen card is dislodged, either by the finger or by the brim of the hat, and it falls in the hat. The pack is placed on the plate, and of course the chosen card is missing to be discovered later in the hat.

34. AN EASY FOUR ACE TRICK

Everyone has heard of the "Four Ace Trick", and here is an easy way to present this mystery.

The four aces are shown in a fan and are replaced on the pack. They are then dealt in a row, and three cards are dealt on each ace.

One ace and its three odd cards are chosen. The magician snaps the other piles and throws them on the table. The aces are gone, and they are found in the odd pile—all the aces together.

The first important part of this trick is the method of exhibiting the aces. They are held in a fan—faces toward the audience; but behind the third card from the front are situated three indifferent cards.

That is, the fan might be: ace of spades, ace of hearts, ace of diamonds, three odd cards, and ace of clubs. The three extra cards are squared up, however, so that they and the ace in front of them appear to be one card. The four aces are exhibited in this fashion, and are placed on the pack and squared up. Then the top four cards are dealt in a row. They are supposed to be the aces, as each card is dealt face down; but only the first card is an ace.

In moving the cards around a bit, the real ace should be allowed to fall from the pack, accidentally, being immediately picked up, the audience, however, catching a momentary glimpse of its face.

Three cards are dealt on each supposed ace, the first three cards from the top of the pack going on the real ace. Those three cards are the three aces; thus the four aces come together, while each of the other heaps holds four indifferent cards. The four heaps are laid in a row, thus:

Four Ordinary Cards	Four Ace Heap	Four Ordinary Cards	Four Ordinary Cards.

A spectator is asked to choose a number *between* one and four. This apparently gives him any choice, but it implies that he should say two, or three. If he says "two", the magician counts from the left of the line; if he says "three", the magician counts from the right, ending his count in either case upon the four ace heap. Should the spectator say "four", the magician replies: "We will use all *four heaps*. Give me another number".

Should the spectator say "one", the magician replies: "We will choose *one heap* from the four. Let me have another number". But the original question invariably eliminates one and four.

All that remains is to command the aces to pass, all four being found in the chosen heap. The magician should do this with much pretence, having a spectator place his hand upon the chosen heap, and snapping each of the odd heaps. He should create the impression that he is doing something really marvelous.

35. THE PADDLE TRICK

The magician shows an ordinary mustard paddle which he lays on the table. A pack of cards is cut, and the paddle is laid between the portions of the pack, after both sides of the paddle have been shown. When the top part of the pack is lifted, a tiny card is seen on the surface of the paddle; and that card corresponds to the bottom card of the upper heap—that is, the card directly above the paddle!

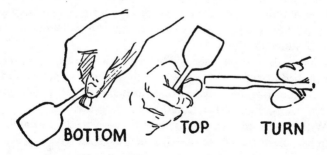

BOTTOM   TOP   TURN

The tiny card, which can easily be made with red or black ink, is affixed to the paddle in the first place. The card that corresponds to it is on the bottom of the pack. The pack is cut; then the paddle is shown apparently on both sides; but in turning the paddle over, it is revolved between the fingers and thumb. (See page 37.) Thus one side of the paddle is shown twice. The magician picks up the *lower half of the pack,* and places it *on the upper,* inserting the paddle between. As he does so, he gives the paddle a half turn, bringing the tiny card upward, directly below the card that corresponds to it.

This trick has a very surprising conclusion; it is not difficult to operate, as the paddle turning is very easy—simply an adaptation on an old trick known as the "Jumping Peg Paddle". It is possible to obtain paddles with rounded handles for this trick, and they revolve very easily.

36. A MYSTERIOUS CARD TRICK

The magician shows his right trousers pocket empty. A card is selected from the pack, and replaced. The magician riffles the pack and asks for the name of the card. When it is given, he reaches into his pocket and brings out two or three cards which reveal the suit and number of the chosen card.

For example: if the three of diamonds is named, the magician brings out the ace of diamonds, giving the suit as diamonds; then he brings out the deuce of clubs, and the total of one and two produce three.

Four cards are concealed in the pocket before the trick. They are pushed up into the corner, so the pocket may be turned inside out without revealing them. These cards are the ace of diamonds, two of clubs, three of hearts and seven of spades.

With these cards it is an easy matter to reveal the suit and the number of any card after its name has been given, for jack counts eleven, queen twelve, and king thirteen.

Thus if the jack of diamonds is named, the magician brings out the ace of diamonds, and says: "Diamond". He follows with the seven, and the three. He adds these three cards and they total eleven, standing for the jack. Had the *queen of diamonds* been selected, he would show the ace of diamonds and toss it aside. Then he would bring out the seven, three and two, showing that those three cards totalled twelve—or queen.

Another example: six of hearts. Bring out the three of hearts, giving the suit. Bring out the ace and two and add the three cards, which total six.

The name of any card in the pack can be revealed in this mysterious manner.

37. CARD AND COIN TRICK

This is a showy little trick—in reality a bit of juggling that looks very difficult yet which can be easily learned.

Balance a card on the tip of your left forefinger. Upon it place a coin—the heavier, the better. With your right forefinger flip the card, and it will sail away across the room, leaving the coin balanced on your finger. This is very pretty and surprising; once you have the knock you can do it every time.

38. THE MYSTERIOUS JOKER

The magician takes a pack of cards and riffles it, holding it in his left hand, while the right hand releases the cards one by one. In this way he shows the backs of the cards—all blue.

Then he turns the pack over and riffles it slowly, looking for the joker. But the joker is not there.

"Strange", remarks the magician. "Let's look through again." He holds the pack faces up and deals the cards one by one. Suddenly he comes to the joker!

He turns the joker over, and its back is red!

Method: Take the joker from a red pack and trim its ends short with a pair of scissors, taking care to round the corners. When the joker is inserted in a blue pack and the front of the cards are riffled, the joker will not be seen, for being short, it falls with one of the other cards.

Likewise when the backs of the cards are riffled, the joker will be invisible, and its red back will not come into view. The appearance of a red-backed joker in a blue-backed pack is very mystifying.

39. CARD CHANGING UNDER FOOT

Show an ace of hearts and throw it face down on the floor, asking a person to put his foot on it. When he lifts his foot the card turns out to be the ace of spades!

Method: Hold the ace of hearts and ace of spades as one, the heart being in front. The fingers are at the back, and the thumb at the front. In throwing the card face down push the back card forward, so that it falls alone. The hand, still in motion, slaps the pack which is in the other hand, leaving the ace of hearts on top. If this is done rapidly, all eyes will follow the falling card and the change will not be detected.

40. UNITED KINGS AND QUEENS

The magician takes the four kings. He states that the pack is a theater, where the kings have arranged a theater party. One king went in the gallery—here he places a king a few cards from the top; while another went in the stage door. Here he inserts a second king a few cards from the bottom.

The other two kings went in the main entrance. Here the magician cuts the pack, drops on the two kings, and completes the cut.

As a result, each king found his proper seat, with his wife waiting for him. Turning the pack faces up, the magician spreads it and shows all the kings and queens together in the center, the king of spades with the queen of spades, and so on.

Method: Place the queen of diamonds on the pack with the queen of hearts above it. On the bottom place the queen of clubs with the queen of spades above it. This is arranged beforehand.

The king of diamonds goes in the gallery. Put the card in the top of the pack, either second or third card down. The king of spades goes in the stage door. Push it in the bottom of the pack, either second or third card from the bottom.

Then cut the pack, and on the upper portion place the king of hearts, and on that put the king of clubs. Complete the cut, putting the bottom half on the top, and the reunion will be completed.

41. THE CIRCLE OF CARDS

There is a very pretty pattern which may be formed with cards, by a very simple method.

Take half the pack and bend the ends inward, very sharply. Bend the ends of the other half outward. Then sort the cards so that they are arranged alternately.

Set the pack on its side, and hold the end closest to you. The cards will spring out and start to form a circle. By carefully arranging their position, you can make them form a neat and artistic circle, which when completed will balance perfectly.

This should be followed by another design, called:

42. THE ROSETTE

This requires the formation of the circle in the manner just described.

While the cards are in the balanced circle, state that you will show a transformation that is very surprising.

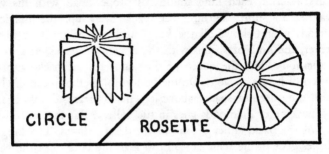

Hit the table, and the cards will fall, evenly distributed, forming a neat rosette.

43. THE CARD FINDER

Here is an easy and effective method of discovering a chosen card.

Run through the pack, and quickly place a number of cards of one suit in a group at the center.

Let a person select a card. Then fan out the pack, and have him replace it near the center. After the pack is squared up and cut twice, you can immediately find the chosen card when you look through the pack. The card *is not taken from* the center but *is put back in* the center.

44. RISING CARD FROM CASE

By this method, the magician can make a playing card rise from the case. It can either be a joker, ace of spades, or some outstanding card, or it can be a chosen card, which the magician has learned by the method just described.

The pack is put in the case, and the case is shaken up and down, the cover being turned back. The desired card will rise.

The trick is accomplished by simply shaking the pack up and down in the case. This action will cause a card to rise. The magician should experiment and discover which card rises in the particular case he uses. It may be the bottom card, the second from the bottom, or even the top card. He places the desired card at the proper position before he puts the pack in the case.

45. REVEALING THE CARD

A pack of cards is shuffled, and five cards are dealt faces up on the table. A spectator is told to choose one mentally. Then the magician picks up the cards, turns his back for a moment, and studies the cards. He turns around, and states that he can reveal the chosen card. He asks the person to name it.

"Five of hearts", is the reply.

The magician instantly cuts the pack to the five of hearts.

Method: When the magician turns around, he has memorized the five cards. He puts one on top of the pack, one on the bottom, two in the center, leaving the deck slightly broken between them, and he slips the fifth card into his pocket.

He does not know the chosen card, but he tells the spectator to name it for the benefit of the other people, so that they can see the trick actually performed.

If the chooser names the card that is on top of the pack, the magician tells him to look at the top card. If he names the card on the bottom, the magician turns up the pack revealing that card. If he names one of the two cards in the middle, the magician quickly cuts the pack at the break*, and shows the card

* The break between the sections is formed by simply laying the upper section at a slight angle upon the lower. This is never noticed, as the pack is not too well squared; but it serves as a guide to the magician and enables him to cut there instantly.

above the cut *or* below the cut as the case may be. If he names the fifth card, the magician takes it from his pocket, and demonstrates that it is the only card he removed from the pack. In any event the discovery is effective.

46. TWO PACKETS

A person takes a small packet of cards, and the magician also takes a small packet.

"Count your cards", says the magician. "If your total is odd, my cards will make it even; if your total is even, mine will make it odd".

The person counts his cards, and the magician adds his packet. The spectator's total is immediately changed from odd to even, or from even to odd as the magician predicted!

Simply deal yourself an odd number of cards, and the trick is sure to work. Odd plus odd will produce even; even plus odd will be odd. Thus you are sure to change his total!

47. RED AND BLACK

A pack of cards is shuffled by the audience. The magician takes it and deals it into two heaps. When they are turned up, the reds are in one pile, the blacks in the other!

Method: Obtain two packs of cards that have the same pattern, but one with cushion finish and the other without.

The cards will look exactly alike. Make the red cards smooth ones, and the black cards rough ones. In dealing, you can tell which is which every time you touch a card.

48. THE ELUSIVE CARD

Two packs of cards are used in this trick. We will call one the blue pack, the other the red.

CARD TRICKS

About a dozen cards of the blue pack are spread around the table, all mixed together, but each card being partly visible.

Each person is given a card from the red pack, and is told to see if his card is in sight among the blue cards spread on the table. One or two persons will say "No", and they are eliminated; but finally a person sees his card in view, so he is chosen for the trick.

He shows his card to other people, and they verify the fact that it is present in the blue cards mixed on the table.

The magician picks up the dozen blue cards, and riffles them. He deals them faces up. The chosen card is gone! The magician immediately produces it from his pocket!

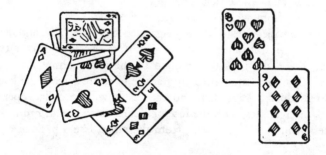

Method: The chosen card is the six of hearts. The blue cards that are spread on the table are carefully arranged. A nine of diamonds is laid face up, and also an eight of hearts. The lower right corner of the nine overlaps the upper left corner of the eight. Thus the nine-spot in the corner and the heart in the corner of the eight make an index of the six of hearts.

Other cards are spread all around these, overlapping in such a way that the join is cleverly covered. The pretended 6 shows, also the heart and the two side hearts of the eight. Anyone will suppose that the six of hearts is on display.

The real six of hearts, however, is in the magician's pocket!

On top of the red pack, the magician places cards that *are not* on display among the blues, with the one exception of the six of hearts. Thus the only person who can possibly see his card on display is the person who holds the six of hearts!

He sees his card there—at least he thinks he does—but as soon as the cards are picked up the elusive six of hearts dissolves. When the cards are dealt, the eight of hearts and the nine of diamonds appear; but no six of hearts. It is in the magician's pocket and is produced from there!

49. CARDS TO CIGARETTES

The magician takes some cards, and deals a few of them on the table. He takes those that remain and changes them to a pack of cigarettes, from which he extracts a cigarette!

Open a paper pack of twenty cigarettes, very carefully, and bend the flaps up. Cut out part of the back of the pack, and paste two cards there, the flaps that remain of the back coming between them. The cards are pasted so that the faces are toward the back.

Press this package flap, and the result will be a flat, opened pack of cigarettes, with the face of a card on the back. From one side it will look like a card; from the other, like a pack of cigarettes.

Put a few cigarettes in the pack, and hold it so people can see the card side, but with several cards in front of it.

Toss the cards off until you come to the fake. Hold your right hand in front of it, and quickly reverse it with your left thumb. Take your hand away, and there is the pack of cigarettes, from which you can shake a few cigarettes.

Then put the package in your pocket.

50. FORCING A CARD

Here is a simple and effective method of making a person take a desired card.

The pack is given to a person and he is told to count off any number of cards one at a time. He does this and is then told to replace the cards on the pack—say twelve.

Another person is told to verify the count. He does so, and when he reaches twelve he is told to look at the card and remember it.

When the first person counted the cards, he reversed their order. So when the second person counted them, he ended on the card that was originally the top card!

So all the magician had to do was start with the desired card on the top, and he knew that that card would be the chosen one!

The magician can hold the pack to his head and name the forced card in a mysterious manner, thus concluding an effective trick. Or he can perform one of the following tricks:

51. THE CARD IN THE WATCH

The magician opens a gold watch with a double back and asks a person who has selected a card to look at the inner back. To his surprise the person sees the image of the card he chose, faintly shining on the case of the watch!

Method: Prepare a tiny card not more than an inch high, and stick it on the inside of the outer case. Force that card from an ordinary pack in the manner previously explained. Then open the outer case of the watch and hold it at an angle. The image of the chosen card will be reflected on the inner case.

With a little practice the magician can secretly introduce the tiny card into a borrowed watch, and deftly remove it with the tip of his moistened forefinger, after the trick has been concluded.

52. A SURPRISE

The magician takes two cards from the pack and puts one in each trousers pocket. A spectator chooses a card. Suppose it is the nine of clubs. Without looking at the card, the magician draws the cards from his pockets. One is a nine, the other is a club.

Method: Have the pack shuffled, and run through it noting the top card. Take two cards that correspond to it, as a jack and a diamond for the jack of diamonds, or whatever the case may be.

Then force the top card by the counting method described previously in this chapter and the trick will work itself!

CHAPTER III

CHECKER TRICKS

Checkers are common objects that are suited to many impromptu tricks; yet somehow they have been neglected in the past. There are, however, quite a few good checker tricks in existence, and some of them are explained in this chapter.

Every household has its checker-board and set of checkers. They are inexpensive articles that can furnish many minutes of diversion and entertainment.

1. THE MAGIC KNOCK–OUT

Ten checkers are stacked up, and all are red except the fourth from the bottom, which is black.

The magician stands another checker on edge, and by pressing down with his finger, snaps it so that it shoots rapidly on edge against the stack of checkers.

Instead of the stack falling, or the bottom checker going out, the one black checker, fourth from the bottom, flies from the stack, while the other checkers do not fall.

This is a very surprising experiment, and it is hard to believe, even after one has seen it performed. It is becauses the black checker is just high enough to receive the blow from the edge of the checker.

Note: If unusually thick checkers are used, it is possible that the third checker from the bottom may be the one ejected. This can be determined by experiment, and the black checker should be placed at the proper position.

2. THREE IN A ROW

Lay three checkers in a row, a black between two reds. Then ask someone to move one red one so that it comes between the other red and the black; yet the second red checker must not be touched, and the black checker must not be moved!

These conditions make the trick sound impossible; but the procedure is very simple.

Place a forefinger on the black checker, and with the other hand slide the first red checker forcibly against the black. The blow will cause the second red checker to slide away, although the black checker is not moved.

Then the first red checker may be placed between the second red and the black.

3. MAKING KINGS

The magician lays ten checkers in a row, and starts to make kings in a peculiar fashion.

He lifts one checker, passes it over two, and sets it on the next checker. He lifts another, passes it over two and sets it on the next checker, and continues thus until he has made five kings with ten checkers.

He must always pass the lifted checker over two, whether those two are separate or have been made into a king.

People who try to duplicate the quick and certain moves of the magician will generally make a mistake before they accomplish the trick.

Here are the correct moves: Pick up 4 and pass it over 3 and 2 setting it on 1; 6 over 7 and 8, placed on 9; 8 over 7 and 5, placed on 3; 2 over the 3 and 8, placed on 5; 10 over the 9 and 6, placed on 7. The numbers refer to the positions of the checkers in the row.

4. THE MYSTIC NINE

With a number of checkers make a figure 9. At least a dozen checkers should be used.

Tell a person to think of a number which must exceed the number of checkers in the bottom of the figure 9. Then, com-

mencing at the end checker, he is to count mentally up the base of the 9, and around the circle until he reaches the number thought of. Then, starting with that checker, he must reverse his count, this time avoiding the bottom of the 9, and continuing around the circle, until he stops at the number chosen mentally.

This is done while the magician's back is turned, but the magician can immediately point out the checker upon which the count is ended.

Here is the system: If the person counted up to his number, and then back again the way he came, he would end where he began. But instead he takes another course. So the magician simply notes the number of checkers in the bottom part of the 9, and counts that many around the circle to the left of its junction with the base. The person's count will always end on that checker, no matter what number he selects.

The trick may be repeated by changing the number of checkers in the base of the 9.

5. THE MAGNETIC CHECKER

The magician takes a checker and sets it against the door. The checker remains there, and does not fall. Apparently it is magnetized to the door, thus proving that wood is magnetic!

Method: It is best to use a checker with a smooth side for this trick. In setting it against the door, or the wood-work, press it upward, sliding it a short distance. The friction will cause the checker to adhere to the wood.

Do not work this trick on any highly polished wood-work, as it may scratch the surface.

6. THE COLOR CHANGING CHECKER

A stack of about seven checkers is set up with a black checker in the midst of red ones.

The stack is covered with a paper tube; when the tube is lifted, the black checker is gone, and only red ones remain!

Method: Cut a loose ring of black paper that will fit around a checker. ALL of the checkers in the stack are red ones, but the center one has the ring around it, and appears to be black. The stack should be slightly uneven.

The paper tube is used to straighten the stack, and the tube when lifted carries away the black ring inside, leaving all red checkers.

7. MOVING THE CHECKERS

The magician places eight checkers in a row, alternating red and black. He makes four quick moves, moving two checkers at a time, and at the finish, all the reds are together and so are all the blacks!

To learn this quick little trick, number the checkers from 1 to 8, and assume that there are two other spaces, 9 and 10, which are not filled with checkers.

Then move the checkers thus: 2 and 3 to 9 and 10; 5 and 6 to 2 and 3; 8 and 9 to 5 and 6; 1 and 2 to 8 and 9.

All the reds will then be together; and so will all the blacks.

8. ELEVEN OR TWELVE?

Lay three checkers on the table. Pick them up, counting "one, two, three", and lay them down, one at a time, counting "four, five, six". Pick them up, counting "seven, eight, nine", and lay them down counting "ten, eleven, twelve".

This appears quite fair; but when the count is repeated, it ends at eleven instead of twelve, and no one can tell why!

Method: Picking up the checkers, count "one, two, three", and laying them down count "four, five, six". Then pick them up, counting "seven, eight—" but as you pick up the last checker, immediately lay it down as you say "nine". Then follow with the two checkers in your hand, counting "ten, eleven".

This is very deceptive, and it will completely baffle people. When they want to try it, give them the checkers, and they will start the count by laying the checkers one at a time on the table. This means failure, as the checkers must be on the table at the start.

Of course everyone will want to see this trick repeated. To repeat it might give away the secret; so instead, the following trick should be performed:

9. NINE OR TEN?

Three checkers are laid on the table. A person is told to pick them up counting "one, two, three", and to lay them down counting "four, five, six", and then to pick them up counting "seven, eight, nine".

But when the magician counts the checkers, his total is ten!

Method: The magician starts with the checkers in his hand, and lays them down counting "one, two, three". He points at an end checker and says "four", then picks up the other two counting "five—six". He immediately picks up the checker still on the table, saying "seven", and lays down the checkers from his hand, one at a time, counting "eight, nine, ten".

10. RIGHT AND LEFT

Take a piece of paper and on it mark seven squares in a row. Place three black checkers in the three squares at the left, and three red checkers in the squares at the right.

The trick is to transpose the checkers, putting red on the left and black on the right, in accordance with the following rules: black can move only to the right, red only to the left; each checker can be moved only one square at a time; single jumps are allowed.

This is a very perplexing problem, which cannot be performed in less than fifteen moves. There is a system to it, and the magician can execute it quickly and perfectly by following two simple rules: First: Start with any color checker and move it, but after every *single move by one color,* make a *jump with the other color.*

After a jump, *advance with the same color* that made the jump. The positions will indicate whether you must make another jump or just a single move.

After the ninth move, the rules do not apply, but from that point on the moves are easy and obvious.

11. THE VANISHING CHECKER

The magician takes twelve checkers and counts them. He counts them a second time, and asks a person to hold them.

The magician then produces one of the checkers from his pocket, and when the spectator counts the checkers, he finds that he has only eleven!

Method: This is done by a clever method of counting. First count the twelve checkers on the table. In stacking them up, secretly hold one in the right hand, which is closed, only the right thumb and forefinger being extended, to count the stack of checkers.

As the checkers have been counted up to twelve, the counting is now reversed. As each checker is laid in a new stack, it is counted thus: "twelve—eleven—ten—nine—eight—seven——". Then the left hand picks up the remaining checkers, shows them and says—"and five makes twelve". Those checkers are then added to the stack which is held by the spectator.

By this count, *eleven* checkers have been made to appear as *twelve*. The magician puts his right hand in his pocket and brings out the odd checker. When the holder counts his checkers he will be surprised to find only eleven.

12. A TRICK WITH A CHECKER–BOARD

Eight checkers and the checker-board are used in this trick. The object is to lay eight checkers on the board in such a way that no two will be in the same line, vertical, horizontal or diagonal.

People will try this puzzler for a long time with no success; but one who knows the secret can do it in an instant.

Simply remember the following numbers: 5, 2, 4, 6, 8, 3, 1, 7. Note how the even numbers run in rotation.

Place the checker-board in front of you and lay the first checker on the fifth square of the top row; the next on the second square of the second row, and so on, according to your formula. Then the conditions of the trick will be fulfilled.

13. PICKING OUT THE BLACK

All the red checkers are thrown into a hat, along with a black checker—the spectators selecting any black checker that they wish. The magician shakes the hat, and holds it behind his back. Then reaching in, he immediately draws out the black checker from among the red ones.

Method: The magician secretly obtains possession of a black checker. This he holds beneath his fingers which are holding the inside of the hat brim—or the checker can be put beneath the inside band of the hat.

When the hat is behind his back, the magician shifts hands and brings out the duplicate black checker.

He immediately turns over the hat on the table, and lets the red checkers fall out upon the remaining black checkers which are lying there. Thus the original black checker joins its companions, and no one suspects that it was not taken from the hat at all!

14. CHANGING CHECKERS

Two stacks of checkers are used in this trick—one stack red, the other black.

Each stack is wrapped up in a piece of paper, the paper being made into a cylinder which surrounds the stack, and the top being twisted over to hide the checkers from above.

The red stack is placed several feet away from the black, and the magician commands them to change places. When he lifts the paper cylinders, the checkers have obeyed the order, the black being where the red were supposed to be, and vice versa.

Two special checkers are required for this trick. One is red, but with black on the bottom; the other is black, with the bottom colored red. It is best to have the bottoms painted the opposite color, but a circular piece of paper may be glued beneath each checker, instead.

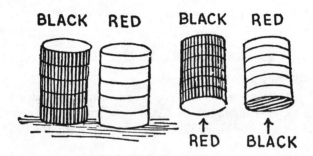

BLACK   RED   BLACK   RED

↑   ↑
RED   BLACK

The prepared checkers are the bottom ones of the stacks. After each stack is surrounded with a cylinder, the magician closes the tops of the cylinders and mixes them around.

Then, to learn which color is in a cylinder, he tilts up the cylinder and lets people glimpse the bottom of the lowermost checker. In this manner, the black stack is identified as red, and the red stack is supposed to be the black.

The magician merely commands, lifts the paper cylinders, and shows the marvelous transposition.

CHAPTER IV

CIGAR AND CIGARETTE TRICKS

1. DISAPPEARING CIGAR BAND

This is a smart little trick that is not difficult. A cigar band suddenly disappears from a cigar, and then comes back again.

Cut a cigar band in half so that only the emblem remains. Glue the half band to a cigar. When the cigar is shown, the band appears to be quite ordinary.

Wave the cigar and give it a half turn between the thumb and forefinger, thus turning the banded side away from view. The band apparently disappears. Another half turn will bring it back. A little practise will make this an effective trick.

2. CIGAR BALANCED ON HAT

Balancing a cigar on a hat is not a difficult trick—when you know the secret! A derby hat is the best to use; but another hat will do. Simply push a pin through the crown of the hat from the inside. Then set the end of the cigar on the pin, and the cigar will balance perfectly on the hat.

In doing this trick, the magician should pretend that it is quite difficult—a feat of genuine balancing. By reaching up inside the hat the magician can remove the pin and release the cigar.

3. THE REVOLVING CIGAR

The magician sets a cigar on its side on the crown of a hat, and flips one end of the cigar. The cigar immediately revolves on the hat, spinning around and around.

As in the last trick a short pin, through the crown of the hat, is responsible. In this case, the side of the cigar, at the center, is pressed on the pin. Hit the end of the cigar and it will revolve on the unseen pivot.

4. THE REVERSING CIGARETTE

A cork-tipped cigarette is pushed through the left fist, the cork tip going in first. When the cigarette comes out the other side, the cork tip comes last.

This is accomplished by cutting the cork-tip from a cigarette, and putting it on a smaller cigarette. Thus the cork-tip will slide freely along the cigarette. When the cork-tip end is pushed into the fist, the fingers retain the tip, and let the cigarette slide through until the end of the cigarette is reached; then the tip is released, so it comes out on the other end of the cigarette.

5. THE MAGNETIC CIGAR

A cigar is laid upon the finger tips of the left hand. The hand is slowly turned over, and the cigar remains there as though magnetized. The hand may be held in any position, but the cigar does not fall until it is removed and laid on the table.

A small pin does the trick. The pin is set with the head between the knuckles of two fingers on the left hand. The cigar is set on the pin point, which projects straight inwards, and it will adhere there.

When the cigar is removed, the fingers are opened slightly, allowing the pin to fall unobserved to the floor.

6. THE INVISIBLE CIGARETTE

This is an interesting pantomime which ends with a trick as the climax.

The magician lays a partly opened box of matches on the

table. Then he pretends to take a cigarette paper from his pocket. He opens an imaginary tobacco pouch and loads the invisible cigarette paper. Then he goes through the actions of rolling a cigarette, which he pretends to place in his mouth.

As if to add a bit of realism to the pantomime, the magician lights a match and holding his hands cupped on account of a pretended wind, he proceeds to light the imaginary cigarette. When he finishes the action, he is smoking a real cigarette, which has appeared from nowhere!

Method: Take a box of safety matches and cut a piece out of one end of the drawer, just large enough to admit a cigarette. Insert a cigarette in the drawer. Push the drawer part way open at the other end and take care that the cigarette is covered with real matches.

Everything is pantomime up until the match is lighted. The box is held in the left hand, and the right strikes the match. As if to avoid a wind, both hands are raised, cupped to the mouth. The left hand pushes the drawer shut, which causes the cigarette to project from the inner end. As the hands reach the mouth, the lips grasp the cigarette. The hands are brought forward a bit so that the cigarette is drawn clear from the box, and the cigarette is immediately lighted from the match. When the hands are lowered, there is the lighted cigarette!

The right hand shakes out the match while the left hand pockets the match box.

7. THE AUTOMATIC CIGARETTE

A pack of cigarettes is held in the left hand. At the magician's command, one of the cigarettes rises out of the pack, of its own accord.

The cigarette is not in the pack at all. It is in back, where it is held by the thumb, which is in the rear of the pack, the fingers being in front, pointing upward.

The back of the pack is pressed in slightly, as the pack is not entirely full of cigarettes. The right hand makes passes above the pack, and the left thumb pushes the hidden cigarette upwards. From two feet away, it appears as though the cigarette is rising from *within* the pack. The right hand takes the cigarette when it has emerged and the pack may then be examined.

This is a very effective little illusion.

8. STRETCHING A CIGARETTE

This is a trick that requires a bit of skill.

A cork-tipped cigarette is taken between the hands, which draw upon it and stretch it to twice its usual length!

Certain brands of cigarettes are made in long sizes, and the magician must obtain one of these long cigarettes. The long cigarette is hidden in the left hand, lengthways, just as the cigar was held in the cigar and pocketbook trick.

The hands then take a normal cigarette of the same brand, and pretend to push it together, as though it were telescopic. In doing this, the cigarette is pushed into the right hand, where it is held by the thumb. The backs of both hands are towards the audience and the finger tips are touching.

The left thumb pushes forward the long cigarette, and the hands begin to draw upon it, instead of the other cigarette. As the hands are gradually pulled apart, the cigarette appears to stretch. When it has finally developed to its full length, it is transferred to the left hand, while the right hand quietly goes to the coat pocket and brings out a box of matches—leaving the original cigarette in the pocket.

As a great many persons are not familiar with the long cigarettes, this trick often creates more than ordinary surprise.

9. THE TIPPY CIGARETTE

A cigarette is placed on the edge of the table so that part of it overhangs. The magician holds another cigarette a few inches below it. As he moves the lower cigarette, the one on the table begins to tip towards it, as though magnetized; and finally it falls off the table, into the outstretched hand.

Magnetism has nothing to do with the trick. It is simply offered as the reason to draw attention from the real method. As the magician leans over the table, he breathes lightly on the extended cigarette, thus causing it first to tip, and finally to fall from the table.

10. THE CIGARETTE IN THE HAND

A cigarette is thrust into the left fist—lighted end first. The magician squeezes his hand until the cigarette is extinguished. Then he opens his fist and shows that his hand has not suffered!

A thimble is held in the closed hand, and it receives the lighted end of the cigarette, which is extinguished when the right hand presses it into the thimble.

As soon as the cigarette is removed—or before—the right hand squeezes the left fist, the right palm being held below the left hand. This is done to "extinguish any sparks". In reality it allows the left hand to drop the thimble into the right, so the left hand can be shown empty, and uninjured.

11. CIGARETTES IN THE CASE

The magician opens a cigarette case and finds it empty. He closes the case, and opening it again, produces two cigarettes from the interior.

The cigarettes are in the case all the time; but they are artfully concealed. The case used is the type that has cross-bands to hold in the cigarettes. One cigarette is laid crosswise under each band. Thus when the case is first opened, it is apparently empty. When

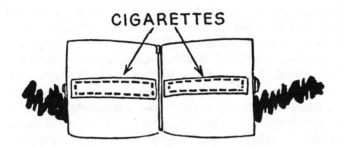

CIGARETTES

the magician opens it again, he can extract the hidden cigarettes, keeping the case away from the spectators so that they will not see the interior.

12. THE RISING CIGARETTE

This is one of the best of cigarette mysteries. A pack of cigarettes is taken from the vest pocket. It opens itself, and a cigarette rises from the interior.

The preparation necessary for this trick is worth the trouble. Make two holes in the side of the pack (which is of the type that slides open) and run a rubber band through, tying knots in the ends. These holes are near the center of the pack, and the rubber band provides the motive power for the self-opening pack.

Remove all wrapping from the pack, so that the cigarettes are loose inside. Take a very short needle, thread it with black thread, and run it through the back of the pack—through both cover and sliding drawer. It should, however, go through the cover at the center, and through the drawer at the bottom. The needle is then pushed point upward into the bottom of a cigarette.

The thread is five or six inches long, and the loose end is wound around a button of the vest. The pack, filled with cigarettes, is placed in the vest pocket.

The operation is not difficult. Remove the pack from the pocket, taking care to push the slide shut. To prevent the slide from opening, press the bottom of the cover firmly between the left thumb and forefinger.

Wave the right hand over the pack, and release pressure with the left hand. The rubber band will force the pack part way open. Continue to wave the right hand, and at the same time move the left hand slowly forward. The thread will become taut and then the cigarette will begin to rise until it is half way out of the pack. Lift out the cigarette with the right hand, and put the pack back in the vest pocket with the left hand.

13. THE NAMELESS CIGARETTE

The magician holds a cigarette between his thumb and forefinger. He shows that there is no name upon it. He raises his hand to show the other side of the cigarette, and there is no name there. But when he tilts the hand forward once more, a name appears printed upon the cigarette.

This is a deceptive trick. In raising the hand up to "show the other side of the cigarette", the magician rolls the cigarette between his thumb and forefinger, giving it a half turn. This motion of the cigarette passes unobserved. Thus both sides of the cigarette are apparently shown, but only one is really exhibited.

The cigarette is then merely tilted forward and the name is seen upon it.

14. THE ANTI–GRAVITY CIGARETTE

A cigarette is laid on the table so that about two-thirds of it protrudes over the edge. Yet the cigarette does not fall!

There are two methods of performing this trick. The first requires a prepared cigarette. A bit of metal is hidden in one end of the cigarette, and as that end is much heavier than the other, the cigarette can easily be set so that it apparently overbalances the table edge.

The trick was improved after further experiment, so that an ordinary cigarette may be used. Simply moisten one side of the tip of the cigarette. Press that side firmly against the table edge, and the cigarette will stick, although more than half of it hangs over the edge of the table.

Do not moisten all the tip of the cigarette as that would give the trick away. Use plain tipped cigarettes in both methods. A cork tip would arouse suspicion.

15.   THE SMOKE TRICK

Drop a cigarette in a glass and put a plate on top of the glass. This will cause smoke to immediately form in the glass, and when the plate is removed, the smoke will pour forth.

Of course it won't work unless you know the secret. Put a few drops of liquid ammonion in the glass; and a few drops of spirits of salts (otherwise known as hydrochloric or muriatic acid) on the plate.

Dropping the cigarette, or half a cigarette, in the glass is just a "bluff". When the plate is put on the glass the acid and the ammonia unite and form smoke—and plenty of it.

16.   SELF–SMOKING CIGARETTE

This cigarette does not actually smoke itself—but it is smoked without the magician or anyone else puffing upon it.

The hands are crossed and clasped together, and the unlighted end of the cigarette is inserted at the base of the thumbs. Then the hands are squeezed together and separated very slightly. This is repeated quickly, and the suction will cause the cigarette to puff furiously, and smoke itself.

The trick may be performed with a cigar or a pipe.

SQUEEZE
HANDS

CHAPTER V

COIN TRICKS

1. MATCH BOX COIN VANISH

A coin is placed in a match box; the drawer is closed and the box is shaken to show that the coin is still there. When the box is opened the coin has disappeared.

The box is prepared by cutting in one end of the drawer a slit just large enough to admit a coin. The opening will not be noticed. When the box is shaken sideways, the coin will rattle; but as soon as you tilt the box towards yourself, with the trick end inwards, the coin will slide out into your hand. The other hand should then take the box and lay it aside, to be opened later.

2. COIN IN BALL OF WOOL

After "vanishing" the coin in the manner explained, you can reproduce it from the center of a ball of wool. To do this, make a flat, stiff tube, of metal or cardboard, through which the coin can slide, and wind the wool around it. When you have secretly gained possession of the coin that was in the match box, turn to get the ball of wool. Drop the coin through the tube, pull out the tube and bring on the ball of wool. Put the wool in a glass; let someone unwind it, and the coin will drop "clink" into the glass. A marked coin should be used.

By using a loose ball of wool, you can work the trick without the tube. The coin is merely pushed through the wool and the ball squeezed around it.

3. RING AND VANISHING COIN

For this trick you require a ring about an inch and a half in diameter. The ring is laid on a piece of paper and is covered with a small square of cardboard. When the ring is set over a coin and the cardboard square is lifted, the coin will be gone. It will come back as soon as the ring is covered and lifted away.

A circle of paper, the size of the ring and the same color as the paper upon which the ring is laid, is pasted to the bottom of the ring. No one observes this, as the disc appears to be part of the sheet of paper. When the ring is placed over a coin, of course the coin will be out of sight.

This trick is rather well-known, so it should be used only as a forerunner to the next trick:

4. THE "WISENHEIMER" COIN TRICK

The effect of this trick is identical to that of the last. A cardboard is set over a ring; the ring is set over a coin; when the cardboard is lifted, the coin is gone. Some "wise" person picks up the ring but finds that there is no paper pasted to it, after all!

Hidden underneath the cardboard you have a little piece of wood, pasted to a strip of cardboard that is as wide as the cardboard square. Thus the little wooden affair can be lifted up with the square of cardboard. The bottom of the wooden piece is dabbed with wax or lead plaster. When the cardboard square is set over the ring, and both are put over the coin, the wooden piece picks up the coin. When the cardboard square is lifted, the coin is taken away and is calmly dropped in the pocket. The person who "knows all about it" picks up the ring and is surprised.

5. THREE APPEARING COINS

Three coins are held edgewise between the thumb and fore-finger of one hand. The coins are overlapping and they are shown on one side—three heads—and on the other side—three tails. The hand shakes the coins, and when it is opened, the three have multiplied to six.

The six coins are there all the time, but the method of holding makes them look like three. On one side are three heads, over-lapping outward; on the other two more coins—tails—overlap outward in the opposite direction. This allows space in between for the sixth coin. When you show one side, and remark, "Three coins heads on this side, and" (turning the hand around) "three tails on this side," every person will believe that he saw the same three coins each time.

6. THE FADE–AWAY COIN

This is a very clever vanishing coin trick. A half dollar is used; and beside the coin you require a small disc of metal, with a hole punched near one edge. The disc is smeared with wax or lead plaster and a piece of cord elastic is hitched to the hole in the disc. The elastic runs up the right sleeve and terminates in a safety-pin. The metal disc should hang just above the cuff, inside the coat sleeve.

To perform the trick, draw the disc from the sleeve and affix it to the half dollar, which is held at the tips of the fingers. The back of the hand is turned to the audience.

The right hand places the coin on the trouser leg, just above the knee, and holds it there, while the left hand folds some of the cloth up over the coin. A standing position must be assumed. As soon as the coin is covered, the right hand releases pressure and the coin flies up the sleeve. Then both hands take hold of the upturned cloth and bend it downwards. Then the cloth is pulled out straight, and the coin is gone.

7. THE WHIRL–AWAY COIN

This is a quick little trick that requires some practice. A coin is whirled in the air and is caught in the right hand, which slaps it on the back of the left.

"Which is it," you ask, "heads or tails?"

As soon as the guess has been made you lift your hand and show that the coin is not there at all.

In "catching" the coin in the right hand, you must hold your fingers straight up, with the back of the hand towards the audience. As the coin apparently falls into your hand, you do not catch it, but let it drop into your coat sleeve. You close your fist, however, and pretend to slap the imaginary coin on the back of your left hand. This is a very effective illusion that is not difficult to perform after a time.

8. THE CHANGING COIN

This is a feat of dexterity that will require careful practice, until the knack is acquired. A person is invited to hold out his hand, flat, with a quarter on the palm. When you strike his palm with your finger tips, he must close his fist immediately, so that you cannot get the coin.

You strike his hand; he closes his fist, and he thinks he has the quarter safe—but when he opens his hand, he finds a five-cent piece instead!

Method: Hold the five cent piece in the crook of your little finger. As you strike his hand sharply with your finger-tips, extend your little finger, letting the nickel fall. The force of the blow will make the quarter bounce, and you may easily catch it as you withdraw your hand from his closing fist.

COIN TRICKS

This must be done very quickly and adroitly but it is not a difficult trick. It simply requires care, speed and precision.

9.   THE MULTIPLYING COINS

Three pennies are laid on the table. Both hands are shown empty. The right hand sweeps the pennies off the table into the left. When the left hand is opened it contains four coins instead of three.

The fourth coin is attached to the underside of the table by a dab of soap. While the left hand is receiving the three coins the left fingers secure the hidden coin and take it along with the others.

10.   ODD AND EVEN

This is more of a catch than a trick; yet it is quite bewildering. A person is asked to take several coins in his hand, and close his fist. Then the magician takes some coins in his hand.

"I will add my coins to yours," announces the magician, "and if you now hold an odd number you will then have an even total. But if you now hold an even number, I will make your total odd."

The person counts his coins, and finds that he has an odd number. The magician adds his, and the total is even, just as the magician stated it would be.

The method is so absurdly simple that very few persons catch on to it. The magician merely has to take an odd number of coins. Then when they are added to the spectator's coins, they will surely make an even total odd, or an odd total even.

11.   THE COIN ON THE DOOR

The magician takes a coin and sets it against the door, where it remains, as though magnetized.

Take a quarter or a half dollar and make two small nicks in the edge, side by side, thus raising a tiny projecting point. When the point is pressed against the door, the coin will stick flat against the woodwork. The little notch will hardly be noticed, but you can knock the coin on the floor, and in picking it up substitute another coin to give for examination. A coin can be borrowed in the first place, and the notched coin substituted for it while you turn to walk to the door.

12.   A COIN BOX

There are various appliances called "Coin Boxes." This one is easily constructed. It may be made from a piece of a cardboard cylinder, or a wooden or metal tube.

A little cylindrical box is shown and is filled with half a dozen coins of the same size. The box, still filled with coins, is set on the back of the left hand. The right hand covers the box, and presto, the coins disappear. The right hand and the box are both shown empty. The left fist is opened, and there are the coins. They have apparently passed through the back of the hand.

Method: The box is nothing but a cylinder. The bottom is a coin which is wedged in place. On the inside of the box, the coin is covered with a disc of paper to make it appear as the inside of the box.

The box is filled with coins. It is set on the palm of the left hand, and is secretly turned over. The spectators see the coin that forms the bottom of the box, and so they think they are seeing the top coin of the stack.

The right hand lifts the box and of course the coins remain in the left hand, which is immediately formed into a fist and is turned back up. The box is set on the back of the hand, and the people still think it is filled with coins.

In passing over the box, the right hand inverts it, so the box appears to be empty. The right hand picks up the box and sets it on the table, and the left hand opens to reveal the missing coins.

13.   WHERE IS THE COIN?

Three little covers, such as the tops of pill boxes, are needed in this trick.

A half dollar is laid on the table, and anyone is invited to cover it with one of the covers, the other two covers being laid beside it so that the magician cannot tell which cover is over the coin. Yet when he passes his hand over the covers, he immediately names the one that conceals the coin.

Method: On the underside of the half dollar a short hair is affixed by means of a piece of wax. No one will observe the hair, because no one is looking for it. The hair protrudes from under the cover which is over the coin, and by looking closely, the magician can discover the location of the coin.

14.   CATCHING THREE COINS

This is a feat of jugglery, but there is a trick to it. Three coins are laid on the back of the right hand. They are tossed in the air, and the hand catches the falling coins, one by one.

Spread out the coins, the first at the finger tips, the second at the middle of the hand, the third at the wrist. Tilt the fingers upwards, in tossing the coins, and they will come down separately, not all at once, and by quick work each coin may be caught individually, with a throwing motion of the hand.

Practise with two coins at first. Persons who do not know the secret will be unable to catch two coins separately.

15. COIN VANISHES FROM HANDS

A coin is laid between the palms of the hands, which are rubbed together. The coin disappears, but comes back when the hands are rubbed once more.

Fix a dab of soft soap to the bottom of the coin. Lay it on the left palm. The right palm is laid crosswise upon the left, and the right fingers push the coin over in back of the left hand. The fingers hide the coin, and they press it firmly against the back of the hand so the palms of both hands may be shown.

To bring the coin back, put the hands together, and this time the fingers of the right hand draw the coin back from its hiding place.

16. HEADS AND TAILS

Lay eight coins in a row, alternately heads and tails. The trick is to move two coins that are side by side to a new position in the row. This maneuver may be done four times, after which the four heads must be together, and so must the four tails.

Method: Counting from the left, move coins 2 and 3 to right end of the line. Then count from the right and move coins 5 and 6 to the vacancy created by the first move. Counting from the right, move coins 2 and 3 to the new vacancy. Then take the two coins from the left end of the line and slide them into the latest gap. The four heads will be together; likewise the four tails. Practise these moves and no one will be able to duplicate them.

17. THE MARKED COIN

A coin is marked with a pencil and is dropped in a hat along with a number of other coins of the same value. When you reach in the hat, you immediately bring out the chosen coin, although the hat is held behind your back.

When the coin is being marked, you ask that a number of people examine it. As they do so, their hands make the coin warm. The other coins will be cold so it is a simple matter to pick out the chosen coin.

18.   COIN, CARDS, AND RINGS

A coin is laid on the table and two cards are dropped upon it. Two metal rings of the merry-go-round type are also lying on the table. The magician puts one ring on top of the two cards and slides the card and ring across the table, leaving the coin beneath the other card. He sets the other ring upon that card.

But when he lifts the card and ring that cover the coin, the coin is gone; and when the other card and ring are lifted, there is the coin!

Method: A hair is attached to one ring and runs to the coin, being affixed to the under side by a dab of lead plaster. The coin and ring lie close together on the table. The two cards are laid over the coin. (The cards are humped up in the center). The attached ring is placed on top, and the hair thus runs under the cards to the end and over to the ring. Take hold of the upper card and slide it away, pushing it *against* the hair. The coin will slide along, unseen beneath the upper card. Cover the lower card with the loose ring and finish the trick.

19.   COIN THROUGH THE TABLE

Four coins are laid on the table. The left hand picks up one and goes beneath the table. The right hand covers the three remaining coins. Then the left hand comes up and drops *two* coins on the table. The right hand is lifted, and there are only two coins beneath it!

Method: An extra coin is used, held concealed in the left hand or stuck under the table with a bit of soap. That accounts for the appearance of the extra coin in the left hand. To make one of the right-hand coins vanish is simple, but clever. The right hand pushes the three coins forward on the table, but in so doing, releases one coin, so that it lies under the wrist. When the right hand is lifted, only two coins remain. The wrist is held flat on the table, hiding the third coin, and by drawing the wrist slowly backwards the coin is allowed to fall in the lap, which should contain a handkerchief or a napkin to catch the coin.

20. HEADS OR TAILS

A coin is laid heads up in the palm of the right hand, which slaps the coin on the back of the left hand. Of course the coin is turned over and now lies tails. But the next time you start with the coin heads up, it still lies heads when slapped on the left hand. In fact, you can start it with either side up and make it come up anyway you choose.

The trick is undetectable. If you turn the hand over naturally, the coin will always turn over with the hand. But if you give the coin a tiny toss and then turn the hand quickly, the hand alone will turn. The slight toss given the coin is impossible to see, as you do it while starting to turn the hand. The trick is very easy to learn and the knack is often acquired the first time a person tries it.

21. THE COIN IN THE KNOT

A handkerchief is twisted in a *rope-wise* fashion. The center is then tied in a knot, and the handkerchief is given to someone to hold. The magician makes a coin disappear; when the handkerchief is untied, the coin is discovered in the knot!

Method: The coin is a duplicate, which is held in the fingers of the right hand. When the handkerchief is twisted *rope-wise*, it forms a sort of tube, sagging in the middle. The magician releases

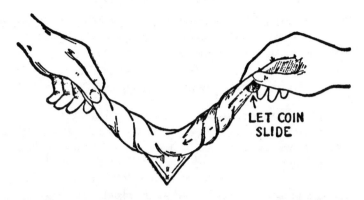

LET COIN
SLIDE

the coin and lets it slide down inside this tube so that it secretly comes to the center of the handkerchief, where it is when the knot is tied.

22. "VANISHING" COIN FROM HANDKERCHIEFS

This is a good method by which a coin may be "vanished" in connection with the trick just described. A coin is pushed down into the center of a handkerchief; when the handkerchief is shaken, the coin has disappeared.

The magician holds one hand beneath the center of the handkerchief. Around the thumb and forefinger of that hand he has a stout rubber band. The coin is pushed down into the rubber band, which is released so that it grips the cloth and forms a pocket. The handkerchief may be shaken but no trace of the coin will remain.

23. THE MISSING COIN

The magician holds out his left hand. He takes a coin in the right hand and slaps it against the left hand two or three times. Finally both hands are shown empty.

In raising the right hand for the last slap, the coin is dropped in the hair. Or, if the magician is wearing a hat, the coin can be left on the brim of the hat. If this little trick is practised a few times it will be found to be a capital mystery.

24. COIN, GLASS, AND PLATE

A glass is inverted on a plate. The magician takes a paper or cardboard cylinder, drops a pencil through it, and puts the cylinder over the glass, which it just fits. Then a half dollar is dropped in the top of the cylinder. It falls on the glass. But when the cylinder is lifted the coin is gone. The glass and plate are raised, and there is the coin, beneath the plate!

A duplicate coin is used, and is previously hidden under the plate. The trick lies in the cylinder, which has a partition of paper, with a small hole in the center which lets the pencil fall through. When the glass is covered with the cylinder, the paper partition fits against the top of the glass so that the coin, when dropped in, is heard to strike the glass. When the cylinder is removed, the coin goes away with it. The cylinder may be made very easily, and should be very plain in appearance.

25. A COIN JOKE

This little trick should be performed on a wooden table or window sill. The magician has a coin which he is changing from hand to hand. Finally he extends his right hand and says, "take the coin," at the same time clicking it down on the wooden table. When the person reaches to take the coin, it has disappeared!

The coin is simply retained in the left hand, which rests on the table away from the extended right hand. When the right hand pretends to lay down the coin, the left hand clicks it against the table. The sound is illusive and the coin seems to be in the right hand.

26.   A QUICK COIN VANISH

A coin is borrowed and taken in the right hand, which makes a throwing motion. The coin immediately disappears.

For this trick, you require a hooked metal clip; several types of these clips are made, and they are sold in stationery stores for hanging up cards etc. The clip has a clamp which will hold the coin, and the hook is on the side.

Borrow a coin, clamp the clip on it, and stand with your right side away from the audience. When you make the tossing motion, drop your hand to your side for an instant, and you can hook the coin on your coat without the least bit of hesitation. Then make the tossing motion and show the hand empty.

27.   THE TALKING COIN

A coin is dropped in a glass; the lights are dimmed, and the coin begins to "talk" by jumping in the glass. One jump means "yes;" two mean "no." After the coin answers some questions, it suddenly leaps out of the glass. Everything may then be examined.

Method: Attach a fine black silk thread to the coin by a dab of lead plaster. You have the other end of the thread beneath the table, and every time you pull the thread the coin jumps. At the finish, give the thread a hard sudden pull; the coin will jump out of the glass and will fly clear of the thread.

28.   BOX AND COIN TRICK

A coin is dropped into a cylindrical box. The coin is shaken to show that it is there, but when the box is opened the coin has disappeared.

The box is just the diameter of the coin, and it should be rather deep. It may be made of cardboard or metal. Adhesive tape boxes will answer the purpose. The box is colored on the inside preferably black; and a piece of paper of the same color is pasted to one side of the coin. The other side of the coin is shown, but when the coin is dropped in the box, it is turned over, so the box will appear empty, the coin seeming to be part of the bottom.

29. THE COIN THROUGH THE SLEEVE

The magician drops a coin down his left sleeve, and pulls the coin through the sleeve at the elbow. There is no hole in the sleeve, so the coin has apparently passed through the cloth.

Two coins are used. One is hidden behind the sleeve by being wedged between the button at the cuff. The hand drops the first coin, and then, reaching behind the sleeve, draws the duplicate down to the elbow.

30. THE COIN AT THE ELBOW

There is an old trick of rubbing a coin into the left elbow, with the right hand. After considerable rubbing the coin disappears. This is done by dropping the coin "accidentally;" in picking it up, the left hand takes the coin, and the right hand pretends to hold it and rubs the imaginary coin into the elbow.

Here is a new addition to the older trick. After the coin has been rubbed away, the right hand rubs the elbow once more. The left arm is held straight upwards, and is twisted so the back of the wrist is toward the audience.

The right hand keeps rubbing the left elbow, until only the heel of the hand is touching it. The fingers and palm are extended off in back of the left arm. At that point, the fingers of the left hand open slightly and let the coin slip out. It drops in back of the left arm and falls into the right hand. Then the right fingers slowly draw the coin out from the elbow.

Worked in combination, this forms an excellent finish to the old trick; for the coin is first "vanished" at the elbow, and is then caused to reappear.

31. AN APPEARING COIN

This is a very clever little coin trick.

A handkerchief is shown absolutely empty. It is rolled into a ball and given to a person to hold. A dime immediately appears in the center of the handkerchief.

Use a handkerchief with a very broad border. Take a few stitches out of the border and there will be a pocket to hold the coin. This side of the cloth is downward when the handkerchief is shown. When the handkerchief is rolled up, the coin slides out of the pocket and into the center of the handkerchief.

32. A BALANCED COIN

A coin is balanced on the magician's forehead—apparently a very difficult feat.

Before the trick is shown, take a dab of wax or soap and attach it to the end of a hair near the front of the head. In setting the coin on edge on the forehead, attach the wax to it. The hair will serve as an invisible line which makes it possible to balance the coin by tilting it slightly forward.

33. THE COIN ON THE FOREHEAD

This is an amusing trick. The magician places a coin against his forehead, and it remains there, as though magnetized.

Simply place the coin against the forehead and push it upward about an inch, using plenty of pressure.

The coin will remain there of its own accord.

34. THE BOUNCING COIN

A coin is thrown on the floor. It immediately bounces up to the magician's hand.

This is accomplished by throwing the coin so that it revolves like a wheel and strikes squarely on its edge. It will then bounce right up, especially if thrown on a stone floor.

The coin must be thrown with considerable force.

35. AN OBEDIENT COIN

A glass is set upside down with two half dollars supporting it, and a dime is pushed beneath it.

The magician states that he will cause the coin to come out from beneath the glass.

He does this by scratching the table-cloth near the glass, the action causing the coin to slide out from beneath the tumbler.

36. TRAVELING COIN

The magician borrows a coin, which he places beneath his left foot.

When he raises his foot, the coin has disappeared, and it appears beneath the magician's *right* foot.

This trick should be performed when seated. Two coins are used. One is secretly placed beneath the right heel. The magician may lift his right foot slightly and draw it backwards without revealing the coin. When he takes the first coin, he pretends to place it beneath his left foot, but drops it in his trousers cuff en route—a very simple yet effective action. Then the coin passes from the left foot to the right, both feet being raised to show the accomplishment.

37. COIN AND PINS

This is a very clever little trick that requires practice. A coin is laid on the table, and the magician, taking two pins, lifts the coin with them, the points pressing against the edge of the coin.

Then the magician blows upon the coin and it revolves between the pin points.

Be sure to use a coin with a milled edge; otherwise the trick will be nearly impossible. With the proper coin, it can be readily learned.

38. COINS FROM ELBOW

Bend the right forearm back until the hand touches the neck, the elbow being quite level. With the left hand, place a stack of coins upon the right elbow.

Then swing the right hand straight down, and catch the coins as you do so.

This looks very difficult—but it is quite easy. Try it with one coin, and the method will be obvious.

39. A COIN DISAPPEARANCE

This trick should follow the one just described. Having shown how coins are caught from the elbow, the magician offers to dem-

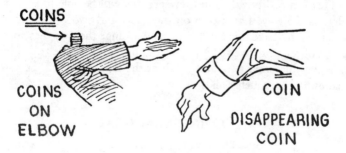

COINS

COINS
ON
ELBOW

COIN

DISAPPEARING
COIN

onstrate the effect with a single coin. He does so, apparently catching the coin in the right hand, but when the hand is opened, the coin has disappeared!

Method. Bend back at the right coat sleeve, to leave the hand free. Place the coin somewhat below the elbow, so it is close to the turned back sleeve. Swing the forearm downward—but not too rapidly. The coin will slide into the fold of the sleeve instead of going into the right hand.

40. FIVE COIN PROBLEM

Take five pennies, and propose the following condition: The coins must be placed in such a way that each coin touches all the remaining coins!

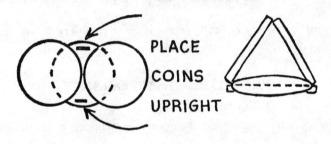

This is a real puzzler, and few persons will be able to solve it. Here is the way: Lay a coin on the table, and two coins side by side upon it. Take two more coins and arrange them so they form a sort of tent, or inverted V, upon the first coin. These two coins ride over the other two, and touch at the top, and it will be seen that every coin touches all the others.

41. COIN FROM GLASS

A tapering, goblet type of glass is needed in this trick. A dime is dropped in the glass, and a half dollar is placed above it. The object is to remove the dime without touching the half dollar.

The trick is only possible with a glass of the type described; for the dime must be a half-inch below the half dollar. Simply blow down the edge of the inside of the glass; that will cause the half dollar to tilt upright, and the force of the blow will make the dime fly up past the half dollar and out of the opposite side of the glass.

42. A COIN CATCH

Two coins are laid on the table, some distance apart; and a third coin is laid almost midway between them. The magician then asks people to estimate which two coins are the farthest apart.

People will look at the middle coin, and some will say the middle and the left end, while others will say the middle and the right end. The magician tells them that they are all wrong—the *two end coins* are the farthest apart!

43. VANISHING MONEY

In doing this it is necessary for the magician to extend his right hand, shaking it so that everyone can hear coins jingle within the fist.

He tells someone to hold his right wrist, so that the money cannot escape up his sleeve. But when the right hand is opened, the money has disappeared!

The money is never in the right hand; instead it is in the left. When the magician shakes his right fist, he holds his right wrist loosely with his left hand, and the coins jingle between his left palm and his right wrist. It sounds exactly as though they were in the right hand.

The excuse for the left hand being there is this: the magician says: "Hold my right wrist—just as I am holding it, so the coins can't get up my sleeve."

That gives him the opportunity to remove the left hand, with the coins, the right being shown empty later.

44. COIN AND TUMBLER

The magician lays a coin on the table, and slides an inverted tumbler over it. The coin immediately disappears.

This is an old trick, but an effective one, if properly shown. A piece of white paper is pasted to the mouth of the tumbler. It matches the table-cloth, and is not seen.

When the tumbler is slid quickly over the coin, the coin is obscured by the paper, and immediately disappears.

In itself, this trick is hardly worth while; but used as a means of vanishing in the following trick, it is very good.

45. COIN THROUGH TABLE

A coin is placed upon the table. The magician shows an empty glass and puts it beneath the table. Then he slides a glass over the coin on the table.* The coin immediately vanishes and is heard to drop into the glass beneath the table. The glass is immediately brought out, containing the coin.

Method: A coin is attached beneath the table by a dab of soft soap or wax. The glass is placed beneath the table and is held so that it encircles the coin.

The instant that the coin disappears from the table, the magician slides the glass so that it dislodges the coin under the table, and the coin audibly falls into the glass.

46. COIN FROM CANDLE

This is a quick and effective coin trick.

The magician goes to a lighted candle, and reaching into the flame, quickly produces a small coin.

* This is with the aid of the glass just described. Any other method of vanishing may be used, however.

Take an ordinary candle and cut a slit vertically, alongside of the wick. Insert a dime or a penny in the slit.

When the candle is lighted, and the coin side is away from view, the coin cannot be seen, as it is behind the light, and well imbedded in the candle.

A quick motion into the candle flame enables the magician to instantly produce the coin.

47. SNATCHING THE COIN

A person holds a coin on his outstretched palm. The magician lays his hand palm up upon the spectator's hand, with his thumb pointing toward the person's fingers.

Then the magician states that he can remove his hand and take away the coin before the spectator has time to close his fingers over it!

Of course the spectator doubts this: but when the magician says "Go", and the spectator closes his fingers, he finds that the coin is in the magician's possession.

Method: The magician must be quick; but everything is in his favor; for the spectator cannot close his fingers while the magician's hand is there. At the word "Go", the magician turns his hand vertically, and with the side of his hand (by the little finger), strikes the spectator's hand at the base of the fingers.

This makes the coin bounce, and as the magician draws his hand away he easily catches the coin and takes it along.

The whole operation takes but the fraction of a second, and the spectator is dumbfounded.

48. A QUICK COIN VANISH

This is an excellent method of vanishing a dime or a penny; it requires a slight bit of skill.

The coin is held between the thumb and second finger. A toss of the hand and the coin is gone! A clutch in the air and it is back again.

Set the coin on the side of the second finger, on the upper knuckle, and hold it in position with the tip of the thumb. The

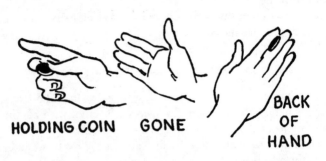

HOLDING COIN   GONE   BACK OF HAND

fingers are bent in—except the forefinger, which is extended so the coin may be seen.

To vanish the coin, place the forefinger over the tip of the thumb; press down, and remove the thumb. Then straighten the fingers showing the palm of the hand. The coin is hidden between the fingers, and it extends in back of the hand.

This must be done very quickly, while the hand makes a quick tossing sweep, ending with the fingers extended and the coin gone. A reversal of the movement brings back the coin.

49. COIN, TUBE AND PAPER

The magician lays a small piece of paper on the table. Above it he holds a coin, horizontally, with his left hand. With his right hand he holds a paper tube to his mouth, the tube pointing straight down on the coin.

Suddenly the paper leaps up and attaches itself to the coin, remaining there for several seconds!

People who try this trick will invariably draw through the paper tube, trying to raise the paper—but the interposed coin will prevent. The real method is to *blow through* the tube, and the paper will jump up to the coin.

50. THE PAPER AND THE COIN

The magician shows a half dollar and a small piece of paper. He states that he will drop both the coin and the paper, and that the paper will fall as rapidly as the coin!

Most people will think this is impossible; but it can be done quite easily. Lay the paper upon the coin and drop the coin flat. The paper will fall with the coin.

The paper, however, should be smaller than the coin.

51. GUESSING THE DATE

This is a tricky problem that is very entertaining. A coin is laid on the table, and the magician allows someone to lay a piece of paper over it. The magician does not see the coin, but he specifies that it must be date side up, as he intends to read the date through the piece of paper.

He states that he will not lift the paper from the coin, but that he will learn the date!

Method: Take a pencil, and rub the paper directly over the coin. This causes an impression of the coin to appear upon the paper, and the date comes into view.

52. HEADS UP!

A half dollar is spun in the air. Every time it falls in the magician's hand, he opens his hand, and the coin is head up. The coin may be a borrowed one.

Method: Have a dime with a dab of wax or double-sided adhesive tape upon it. Secretly attach this dime to the tail side of the half dollar. Spin the coin in the air, and the dime will not be seen. The coin is caught in the hand, and it will generally fall head up; if it does not, the magician can instantly detect it, and turn it over as he opens his hand.

After tossing ten or twelve heads, the magician can secretly detach the dime, leaving it in his hand. while he gives the coin to someone else to try.

53. COIN THROUGH HANDKERCHIEF

A coin is placed in the center of a handkerchief, and its shape is plainly visible. The handkerchief is held in a person's fist, with just the coin showing at the top. Another handkerchief is thrown over it, and when it is removed, there is the coin, while the lower handkerchief is empty.

Method: In putting the coin under the handkerchief, the coin is retained in the hand, and a piece of wire, twisted in a circle, is placed there instead. This is the shape that shows through.

When the second handkerchief is placed over the first, the coin is under it. Then the magician grips the thin wire through the cloth, and pushes one end of it right through the handkerchief, thus drawing the wire through. He lifts the upper handkerchief, revealing the coin, and takes away the wire with the handkerchief. As very thin wire is used, only a tiny hole is in the handkerchief, and that will never be noticed.

A marked coin may be used in the trick.

54. TACK IN THE CEILING

This does not start out as a coin trick—but a coin plays the most important part in it.

A thumb-tack is to be driven in the ceiling, simply by tossing it in the air. Everyone wants to see that done, so the magician obliges.

He takes a piece of very thin tissue paper. He lays the tack point up upon a half dollar; then he places the paper over the point of the tack and wraps the paper around the coin.

The package is tossed forcibly against the ceiling, holding the point of the tack upward. The tack is thus driven into the ceiling; then the weight of the coin tears the paper loose and down drops the coin with the paper, leaving the tack up there.

55. COINS, PLATE AND GLASS

Here is a trick that involves the visible penetration of a coin through a china plate.

The magician borrows several coins, a quarter being among them. He sets a plate on a glass, and taking the coins in his right hand, drops them on the plate. The quarter continues right through the plate and falls into the glass.

Method: A duplicate quarter is affixed to the bottom of the plate with a dab of soap or wax. The coin is slightly away from the center of the plate.

The coins are taken in the left hand and dropped into the right, but the quarter is retained in the left hand. This is quite easy to do with so many coins being used. The left hand closes over the quarter, and just the thumb and forefinger are extended. They take hold of the plate "to steady it", the plate having been placed over the glass, so that the coin touches the inner edge of the tumbler.

As the right hand drops the coins on the plate, the left hand draws the plate slightly in the proper direction, releasing the duplicate quarter, which falls visibly into the glass. As no quarter is on the plate and the right hand is shown empty, it appears as though the coin has penetrated the plate.

56. THE HIDDEN COIN

A coin is placed beneath a cup, while the magician is not present. The magician comes back, touches the cup, and immediately names the denomination of the coin.

A confederate helps in the trick. It will be noticed that the handle of the cup can be turned to point in any direction, like the hand on a clock. The confederate looks at the coin beneath the cup, and sets the handle properly, in accordance with the following system: 1 o'clock, a cent; 2, nickel; 3, dime; 4, quarter; 5, half; 6, dollar; 7, $2.50 gold piece; 8, $5; 9, $10; 10, $20; 11, a foreign coin, or imitation; 12, no coin at all.

CUP COVERS COIN

POSITIONS

In this way the magician can name the denomination of the coin, tell whether or not something other than a United States coin is beneath the cup, or whether the cup covers nothing.

57. COIN ON THE WRIST

The magician holds his hand palm up and lays a coin on his wrist. He says that he can make the coin turn over without touching it.

This he does by snapping his fingers. If a dime is used, it will turn a neat somersault when the fingers are snapped. With a little practice the knack can be easily acquired.

58. ODD OR EVEN?

The magician holds several coins in his hand and asks a person to guess whether the money is odd or even. The person is certain to make the wrong guess.

No skill is required. The magician merely uses a dime, a nickel, and five pennies. If the person says "even", the magician opens his hand, and counts the coins, showing that he has seven—an odd number. If the person says "odd", the magician counts the amount; ten cents for the dime, five for the nickel, and five for the pennies, a total of twenty cents, which is even.

59. THE FOUR COIN TRICK

Four coins—all alike—are laid on the table, forming a square. Two playing cards are used, and a coin is covered with each card. Taking an uncovered coin, the magician puts it under the table, or the table-cloth, and when a card is lifted, two coins are there. The two coins are covered, and the other uncovered coin is passed under the card in the same mysterious manner.

Then the three coins are covered. The other card is lifted, and the coin has passed from beneath it, all four coins being found beneath one card.

This trick must be carefully rehearsed; but it is not difficult to perform.

At the outset, the magician is undecided which coins to cover with the cards. He tries the cards over different coins, and this gives him the opportunity to take hold of a coin beneath the card in his right hand.

He lifts the left hand card from a coin, and just as he draws the right hand card away, he drops the left hand card where the right one was, so that nobody notices the absence of the coin. Then he lays the right hand card over another coin, taking care that the coins do not clink. He now has two coins under one card and no coin under the other.

He picks up an uncovered coin, and in putting it under the table or the cloth transfers it to his left hand. He brings out his right hand, empty, and with it lifts the card, disclosing two coins.

The card is transferred to the left hand which is below the level of the table, the coin resting on the left fingers. Then the left hand lays the card on the two coins, adding the third coin to the group.

In the same way the other uncovered coin is "passed" beneath the card, and is added to the group when the card is replaced. That brings four coins beneath one card, while the other card covers none. So the magician makes a mysterious pass, lifts both cards, and shows all the coins together.

CHAPTER VI

CORK TRICKS

1. THE BOUNCING CORK

This is a clever little trick that is quite perplexing.

The object is to drop a large cork so that it will stand upright. Different people try it, but whenever the cork strikes on end, it bounces at an angle and falls over.

The magician, however, can make the cork fall so that it stands on end, even when dropped a foot or more.

The secret lies in the position in which the cork is held. It is dropped so that it falls on its side; then, when it bounces, it will stand upright.

2. UPRIGHT CORKS

The object of this trick is to make several corks float upright in a bowl of water. The corks naturally float on their sides, and it seems impossible to make them float vertically.

Yet the magician can accomplish the feat very easily.

He does this by placing several corks in the bowl together, all upright, in a circular group. The sides of the corks become wet, and they stick together and float upright.

3. TWO CORKS

This trick is always good. Two corks are used and they are set as shown in Fig. 1, one cork at the base of each thumb. Then the fingers and thumbs grip the ends of the corks, and when the hands are taken apart, the corks come away freely, although one would suppose that they would hook together.

In fact, when people try the trick, they will invariably fail, as they make the corks interlock. See Fig. 2.

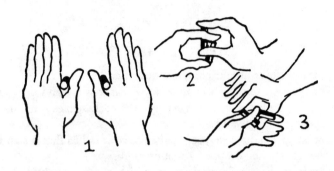

The magician accomplishes the separation thus: He holds his hands back up and places his right forefinger on top of the left hand cork. His right thumb goes on the bottom of the cork. The left thumb extends into the right palm and presses against the bottom of the right hand cork, while the left forefinger bends around and presses the upper end of the right hand cork.

In this position (which is shown in Fig. 3), the corks will apparently interlock and make it impossible to draw the hands apart. But actually the corks are separated, and the hands can be easily taken apart. Large corks should be used.

4. CORK AND BOTTLE

In this trick, a small cork is to be blown into a large necked bottle. This seems very easy, as the cork will slide through the neck of the bottle—but the bottle must be held horizontally, so that the force of a blow will send the cork in.

CORK TRICKS

The person who tries it gives a big puff—and the cork, instead of going in, comes out of the bottle!

This is because of the air in the bottle. The harder one blows, the less chance he has for succeeding.

The correct method is to blow very gently; or to blow the cork through a straw, when it can be propelled into the bottle.

5. ADHESIVE CORKS

The magician takes two corks and places them together, the ends touching. He holds the uppermost cork, and the lower cork remains attached to it.

Other persons, however, will be unable to make the corks adhere.

This is because the magician secretly moistens the top of one cork. Then, when they are placed together, they will adhere.

6. REMOVING THE CORK

This is more of a catch or a joke than a trick; yet it is quite interesting, and is often the cause of much speculation.

A corked bottle is shown, and the bottle is partly filled with liquid. Obviously the liquid cannot be removed unless the cork is withdrawn.

Yet the conditions of the problem, when stated are that the liquid must be removed without damaging the cork or taking it out of the bottle—and without breaking the bottle!

This sounds impossible; but there is a way in which it can be done. The cork is a short one, cylindrical in shape. So the demonstrator *simply pushes the cork into the bottle*. The liquid may then be poured out; but the cork is still in the bottle!

7. THE IMPROVED MULTIPLYING CORKS

This is not a new trick, but an improvement has been added to it which makes it more effective.

A small pill-box is opened and is shown to contain three corks. The cover is put on and the box is shaken. When it is reopened, it is found to contain six corks. These are poured out on the table.

Use a large pill-box, which has a cover identical with the bottom. The "collar" of the box being removable, the top and bottom are reversible.

By the old method, three corks were glued to the inside of the cover; but in the improved version, they are simply stuck there by dabs of beeswax or diachylon (lead plaster).

The box is shown to contain three corks. The cover is put on without showing the interior. The fact that the lid may be lifted thus indirectly proves that it is empty.

Then the box is shaken, and is turned upside down in the action. This loosens the corks from the erstwhile lid; and when the new lid (formerly the bottom) is lifted, there are six corks which can be poured out on the table. If the corks are very lightly attached, the reversal of the box will be unnecessary.

CHAPTER VII

DICE AND DOMINO TRICKS

1. THE MAGNETIC DICE

A pair of dice are placed on the table, and one die is set upon the other. When the upper die is lifted, the lower one clings to it as though magnetized.

Method: Previously moisten the tip of your forefinger, and apply it to the under side of the upper die. When the dice are pressed together, they will stick, and they may be lifted as one.

2. NAMING THE TOTAL

Tell a person to roll a pair of dice on the table, while your back is turned. He must add the total made by the dice. Then he should pick up one die and, turning it over, should add the number on the bottom of the die. Having done this, he must roll the single die and add the number that appears on the top side.

When you look at the dice as they lie on the table, you can immediately name the total that the spectator has reached!

Method: Simply count the spots on the dice as they lie on the table, and add seven to the total. You will then have the grand total. Here is the reason why: The opposite sides of a die always total seven. The roller let one die remain on the table. But when he picked up the second die and added both the top and bottom into his total, he was merely adding on seven. When he rolled the die again, its new number lay there for you to see, along with that of the first die.

3. THE END NUMBERS

Place a set of dominoes on the table, and invite two or three persons to line up the dominoes, as though playing a game; but as the dominoes are all face up, the game can be finished in a few minutes. Before they start, you write something on a piece of paper and lay it where all can see.

When the game is finished, there will be two ends to the row of dominoes. Suppose the end number on one row is five; on the other row, three. When the piece of paper is unfolded, it will bear the numbers five and three. You have foretold what the end numbers will be!

Method: Secretly remove one of the dominoes (not a double) before the game begins. The numbers on the domino (in this case 3 and 5) will tell you what the end numbers will be.

4. THE INCOMPLETE GAME

In this case, two people are invited to play a game of dominoes, but somehow or other they cannot finish it. Several dominoes will be left over.

For this trick, you take away *two* dominoes, bearing four different numbers, say 3—5 and 6—1. If this trick follows the last, simply take away one domino besides the one you already have. The game cannot be completed. As soon as the players have realized this, mix up the dominoes and slip back the two you have taken. Then tell them that the magic spell has been lifted and that they can go ahead without interruption.

5. SIXTEEN DOMINOES

Lay sixteen dominoes in a row on the table. While your back is turned, any person may move as many dominoes as he chooses from the right to the left of the line. The dominoes must be moved one by one, and not more than a dozen may be moved.

When you come back, you immediately turn a domino with the spots up, and the spots on the domino tell how many have been moved!

Method: Arrange the dominoes from left to right so that the spots total 12, 11, 10, 9, etc., down to 0 (the double blank). The three dominoes on the right of the row are odd ones.

Now, if no dominoes are moved, and you turn up the fourth domino from the right, it will register zero—double blank. If one domino is moved, the fourth from the right will be 1; if two are moved it will be 2, etc. Simply turn up the fourth domino from the right of the row.

6. TOTALLING THREE DICE

Place three dice in a tumbler and put your hand over the open end, holding the glass between your palms. Approach a person who is seated, and shake the glass so the dice jump about; then ask him to look up through the side of the glass and count the spots on the bottom of the dice. He has hardly done so before you tell him the total; although you cannot see the bottom sides of the dice.

Method: Add the *top* sides of the dice, which you can see, and subtract your total from 21. That will give you the total of the bottoms.

7. DICE IN CUP

This trick requires a pair of dice and a "shaker" or dice-cup, either the large leather type used with standard size dice, or one of the small cardboard dice-cups that come with parlor games utilizing small dice. If no dice-cup is available, a paper drinking cup can be used.

A pair of dice are dropped into the cup and the magician puts his hand over the mouth of the cup, turning it to create a vacuum. He then inverts the cup and the dice fall out. He tries again and after about the third try, to everyone's wonderment, the dice do not fall, but for some unexplainable reason remain up in the cup.

Pressing his hand to the cup's mouth, the magician turns his hand the other way; this time, when the cup is inverted, the dice drop.

The "vacuum" has nothing to do with it. Beforehand, the magician wedges a wooden match-stick—or a portion of one if a small cup is used—across the interior of the cup, near the bottom and toward one side.

By simply tilting the cup that direction when inverting the cup, the dice will slide above the wedge and stay there, only to drop later when the cup is tilted the other way. A few "failures" make the trick more convincing and afterward, pressure on the side of the cup will release the match so it can be dropped unnoticed on the floor.

CHAPTER VIII

EGG TRICKS

Inasmuch as Christopher Columbus has been given credit for performing the first known trick with an egg, this chapter will begin with an explanation of how that famous feat might have been accomplished. According to the story, Columbus balanced an egg on end. The trick is a very interesting dinner table experiment, so here are three methods of performing it:

1. THE BALANCED EGG

Method 1. Shake the egg so that the yolk will settle. Then set the egg carefully upon the table, and as the bottom of the egg is heavier than the top, it will be possible to balance the egg on end.

Method 2: Before performing the trick, spill a little salt on the tablecloth and gather it up into a tiny mound. Press the egg carefully on the pile of salt, and it will balance there.

Method 3: Have a tiny ring under the table cloth with a thread attached. Balance the egg by setting it on the ring. When you lift the egg away, pull the thread with your other hand so that the ring will be withdrawn.

2. SPINNING AN EGG

Two or three eggs are laid on the table, and people are asked to spin them. They find that the task is next to impossible. The eggs start to spin, but topple and fall on their sides. But when the magician twirls an egg, it spins like a top.

One of the eggs is hard-boiled. It is kept out of sight until different people are busy spinning eggs; then the magician picks up one of the eggs and takes an opportunity to replace the hard-boiled egg in its stead. The hard-boiled egg may be twirled with ease.

3. THE FLOATING EGG

An egg is dropped into a pitcher of water and it mysteriously floats halfway down, neither coming to the surface nor sinking to the bottom!

This is due to the water in the pitcher. The pitcher is half filled with water, which is then salted. More water is poured in, down the *sides* of the pitcher, so that the bottom half of the pitcher contains salt water and the top half fresh. The egg will then float halfway up.

4. EGGS, SPOOLS, AND GLASSES

This is a very elaborate trick, which can, however, be easily prepared.

Three goblets of water are stood in a row and a thin piece of wood is set upon them. Over each of the two end goblets, a spool is set, and an egg is balanced on each spool.

Over the center goblet, another goblet is inverted; a spool is placed on it, and an egg is balanced on the spool.

The magician suddenly grasps the inverted goblet and pulls it away. The board and the spools fly to the floor; but the three eggs drop squarely into the goblets of water!

On the thin piece of board, there are two tiny projecting nail points, which engage the edge of the inverted goblet in back. These are so tiny that they are not noticeable, but they are very important in the trick. For when the inverted goblet is pulled away, it carries the board also, and the light spools will fly away. The eggs, however, will fall directly down, of their own accord, into the goblets.

5. EGG TO CONFETTI

The magician shows an ordinary egg, and squeezes it in his hand, while he fans it with the other hand. A shower of confetti pours forth, instead of the egg.

The egg is a real one, but it is prepared for the trick. Punch a tiny hole in each end of the egg, and you can blow the contents of the egg out into a cup. Enlarge one of the holes so that confetti may be poured into the egg.

In performing the trick, hold the egg between the tips of the thumb and forefinger, which cover the holes. When the egg is squeezed, the shell is broken, and falls with the confetti, which should be dropped into a box.

Note: See also the "Ring in the Egg," page 186.

CHAPTER IX

HAND TRICKS

There are several tricks in which the hands play a principal part—without serving merely as agencies in the manipulation of other objects. Such tricks are sufficiently numerous to require this separate chapter.

1. THE MUMMIFIED FINGER

The magician exhibits a small cardboard box. He removes the lid, and shows a finger inside, the finger being packed in cotton.

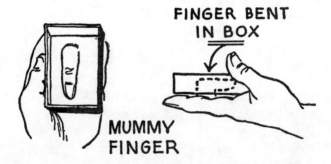

He states that it is a mummified finger; and when someone starts to inspect it closely, the finger suddenly moves.

The finger is the second finger of the magician's left hand.

There is a hole in the bottom of the box, through which the finger is thrust. The box appears to be set on the palm of the left hand. If the finger is covered with talcum powder or chalk, the surprise will be great.

2. THE EXTENDED FINGER

The magician pulls on the forefinger of his right hand, and it suddenly stretches to twice its original length. Then it is restored to its normal size.

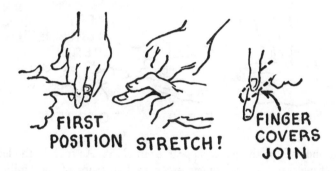

FIRST POSITION   STRETCH!   FINGER COVERS JOIN

The finger is first placed across the knuckles of the first and third fingers of the left hand, with the left second finger over it, resting on the knuckle of the right forefinger.

Then the tip of the right forefinger is turned so that it rests on the knuckle of the left forefinger, both forefingers pointing in the same direction. At the same instant, the left second finger is bent across the nail of the right forefinger. Thus the left forefinger appears to be an extension of the right forefinger. The hands should be kept in motion during this procedure, and finally the fingers are brought back to their original position. This is a very surprising illusion.

3. THE REMOVABLE THUMB

There are variations of the following trick, but the method about to be described is by far the most effective. It consists of the apparent removal of the right thumb from the hand.

The hands are held as shown in Fig. 1. Then the thumb is "taken off" as shown in Fig. 2, and immediately replaced again.

The secret is shown in Fig. 3. The right thumb is bent in, and the left thumb is arranged to form an extension of it. The draw-

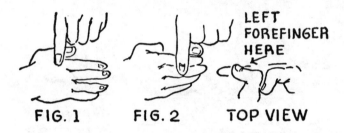

FIG. 1   FIG. 2   TOP VIEW

ing shows how the hands appear from above. As soon as the left forefinger and second finger are placed in front of the "joint", the illusion is complete. The right thumb appears to be naturally extended. (See Fig. 1.) The rest of the right hand may be moved up and down to assist in the illusion. Then the thumb is "removed", and "replaced". The left fingers immediately come down in front of the thumbs, and during the temporary concealment, the right thumb is extended, and the left hand moves away, showing the entire right thumb.

The right thumb may be extended at the beginning of the trick, the left fingers momentarily "covering up" while the thumbs assume the proper positions.

4. THE DETACHABLE FINGER

A similar trick may be performed with the third finger of the left hand. The finger is held as shown in Fig. 1; bent in and held by the left thumb. The third finger of the right hand takes the position shown, and when the first two fingers of the right hand are bent in front, the appearance is shown in Fig. 2.

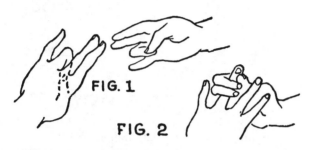

FIG. 1

FIG. 2

The right hand moves sideways, and it appears as though it is bending the left third finger. Then the hand is moved away, carrying the finger, which is immediately replaced. The right hand is quickly turned over, and at the same instant, the left finger is extended, under cover of the right hand.

In both of these tricks, as well as in others requiring movements of the hands, the reader may work the tricks with the other hands, if he finds it more convenient. The usual procedure is to "remove" the right thumb, or the left third finger; but some may find it easier to use the left thumb or the right third finger.

5. STRETCHING THE THUMB

This is a variation of the "Removable Thumb" trick. In this case the magician apparently stretches his thumb to twice its natural length.

The right thumb is bent into the palm and the back of the hand is turned toward the audience. The left thumb is extended, and the back of the hand is also toward the audience.

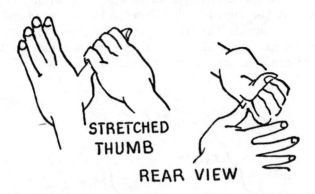

STRETCHED
THUMB

REAR VIEW

The right fingers cover the left thumb, which is pushed between them and the right thumb, but the tip of the right thumb is allowed to protrude alongside the right little finger. It appears to be the tip of the left thumb.

The right hand is moved slowly to the right, and the illusion is created of stretching the left thumb to twice its length. Then the right hand goes back to the left, and the left thumb is shown as good as ever.

6. ELEVEN FINGERS

This is more of a joke than a trick; yet it really mystifies many people. The magician states that he has eleven fingers, counting his thumbs.

Using his right forefinger as a pointer he touches each finger of the left hand, counting "One, two, three, four, five".

Then his left forefinger counts the right fingers: "Six, seven, eight. nine, ten".

"Strange", remarks the magician. "I thought I had eleven. Let's try again".

He starts counting backwards, pointing to the fingers of the right hand. "Ten, nine, eight, seven, six". Then he stops, holds up his left hand, and says: "And five are eleven!"

Executed rapidly, this clever method of counting is very deceptive.

7. FLEXIBLE HANDS

This is something of an optical illusion. The palms are placed together, and are bent back and forth, the fingers being extended. Suddenly each hand seems to bend back almost to the wrist, as though the magician possessed remarkable double joints.

This is accomplished by turning the hands from right to left. As the back of the right hand comes into view, hiding the left hand, the left fingers are doubled slightly, allowing the right fingers to bend over them. As both thumbs are together, the effect is that the left fingers have bent back. A quick turn the other way, and the right fingers double up, letting the left fingers bend over them. This is done after several pretended attempts to bend the fingers back, and it is quite surprising.

8. CLAPPING THE HANDS

Here is a method of clapping the hands without taking them apart. To convince everyone that the hands are not separated, the fingers are locked together. Yet when the hands are moved up and down rapidly, they clap very audibly.

To do this, separate the heels of the hands and bring them together very rapidly, while the hands move up and down to hide the slight motion of them. With a little practice, loud applause may be produced although the hands move less than an inch or so apart.

9.   TOUGH KNUCKLES

A blow on the knuckles is usually quite painful. Yet the magician can strike his knuckles forcibly against the edge of a table without either hurting his hands or the furniture.

Needless to say, there is a trick to it. The knuckles do not touch the table at all. The magician taps them against the edge of the table a few times; then he makes a hard swing, and as his hand is in motion, he extends his fingers, so that the tips and not the knuckles, strike the wood. The hand is immediately doubled up before the swing is completed.

To all appearances, the knuckles have been struck forcibly against the table edge, as everyone can hear the blow.

10.   AN ILLUSION OF TOUCH

By a very simple expedient, it is possible to make a single object, such as a small ball, or a pencil, appear as two.

This is done by crossing two fingers. Then place the ball or the pencil so that it touches the tips of both fingers.

Due to the unnatural position of the fingers, two distinct touch impressions are recorded. If the eyes are shut, or are turned away from the hand, it is difficult to believe that the fingers are touching a single object only.

CHAPTER X

HANDKERCHIEF TRICKS

There are three types of handkerchiefs used in the performance of tricks: First, ordinary linen handkerchiefs, which serve the purpose in most impromptu tricks; second, large thick silk pocket handkerchiefs, which are used in tying knots, as they slide more easily than linen; and third, thin, small silk handkerchiefs which are used in connection with various pieces of magical apparatus.

The impromptu magician would do well to carry a large silk handkerchief in his pocket, as it is useful in many tricks. The sole advantage in the linen handkerchief lies in the fact that it is not so transparent as silk; and sometimes something takes place underneath a handkerchief which the spectators are not supposed to see.

1. THE BALANCED HANDKERCHIEF

A handkerchief is folded diagonally and is rolled into a long cylinder. It is then balanced upright on the tip of the forefinger. The handkerchief sways but does not fall.

This is accomplished by having a piece of whalebone or pliable wire hidden in the folded handkerchief. The handkerchief is rolled around the wire, and it may then be easily balanced on the tip of the finger. The handkerchief should be pocketed immediately after the trick, and brought out later on, minus the wire or whalebone.

2. THE DOUBLING KNOT

Hold a corner of a silk handkerchief in the left hand. Place the right hand, palm up, under the center of the handkerchief. Then roll the right hand over toward the left so that the back of the right hand is up. In so doing the right hand clutches the handkerchief so that a loop is formed. Insert the third finger of the left hand in that loop, from beneath, and withdraw the right hand.

Move the right hand further down the handkerchief and form another similar loop. Place it on top of the first loop and hold the two loops pressed together by the right hand.

Then the left hand pushes the left end of the handkerchief up through the two loops, forming two knots, one upon the other. Spread the upper knot so that it surrounds the lower. Then take hold of the left end of the handkerchief and let the handkerchief dangle. To all appearances there is a large single knot in the center of the cloth. Give the silk handkerchief a sudden snap, and instead of the one knot, there will be two knots, a few inches apart.

3. THE APPEARING KNOT

A handkerchief (linen or silk) is held in the right hand by one corner. Attention is called to the loose hanging corner. The loose corner is raised to the right hand, which drops it with a shake, still retaining the upper corner. This is repeated several times, and suddenly a knot appears in the hanging corner.

Method: The corner originally held in the right hand is previously knotted but the knot is hidden by the fingers. After raising and shaking out the hanging corner two or three times, the right hand exchanges the corners, retaining the lower one, and letting the knotted one drop. This is a perfect little illusion and it seems as though a knot suddenly appears in the loose corner.

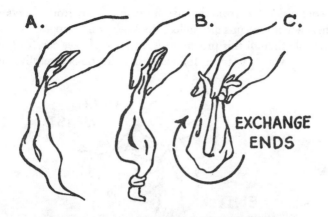

4. NON-BURNING HANDKERCHIEF

Drawing a handkerchief through a candle flame is a very mysterious trick. It may be done by simply rolling the handkerchief into a cylinder and drawing it through the flame slowly, but without stopping at any point. If, however, the handkerchief has been previously soaked in a solution of borax and water, it will be rendered nearly fireproof, and the trick can be performed with more deliberation. The handkerchief should be allowed to dry before it is used. The handkerchief can be held by the upper corners while the lower edge is drawn through the flame.

5. THE FLYAWAY KNOT

This is one of the most deceptive of all handkerchief tricks. A handkerchief is apparently tied in a knot, but the knot dissolves when the ends of the handkerchief are pulled.

The method of tying the knot is not difficult. Hold the handkerchief by diagonally opposite corners. The right hand then carries its end away from the body and over the left wrist. The right hand end is then thrust through the loop thus formed from

the outer side (i.e. from the side of the loop away from the body).
Then when the ends are pulled, the knot will disappear.

Simple though this procedure is, it is not always easy to learn.
The only way is to try it, following the directions carefully, until

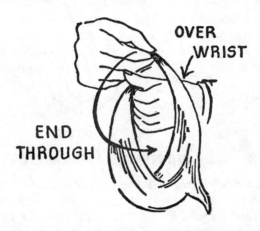

you finally succeed, which may be on the first attempt. Once acquired, the trick can be performed very rapidly.

6. THE DRAW–AWAY KNOT

A loose knot is tied in the center of a handkerchief. The left
hand holds the upper corner of the handkerchief, and the right
fist is drawn down over the knot two or three times. On the
last attempt, the hand draws the knot right out of the handkerchief! Persons who attempt to duplicate this trick will find that
their efforts only serve to tighten the knot.

That is because there is a very clever trick to it. When the
right hand is finally drawn over the handkerchief, the fist does
not grip the knot at all. Instead, one of the fingers of the right
hand is hooked into the knot, as the hand sweeps downward.

The finger will pull the knot right down and out of the cloth. Use a silk handkerchief and do not tie the knot too tightly.

7. UNITED AND UNTIED

Two handkerchiefs are shown separately. They are tossed up in the air and they come down tied together. The left hand holds the upper handkerchief with the lower one dangling. The right hand sweeps down over the handkerchiefs and they fall apart.

Method: Have a rubber band on the tips of the right thumb and forefinger. In tossing the handkerchiefs into the air, slip the elastic over one end of each handkerchief and when they come down they will seem to be tied. When the right hand sweeps down it simply pulls the lower handkerchief and the "knot" is gone. The elastic is secretly dropped on the floor.

8. MATCH IN HANDKERCHIEF

A match is placed in the center of a handkerchief. The match is broken through the cloth, but when the handkerchief is unrolled, the match drops out, uninjured.

A duplicate match is concealed in the hem of the handkerchief. This is the match which is broken through the folded cloth —not the original match.

By having a second match concealed in another part of the hem, the trick may be repeated. The hidden matches should be near corners of the cloth.

9. THE DISAPPEARING HANDKERCHIEF

This is a most mystifying trick which can, however, be shown to only one person at a time. Use a very small handkerchief. This you roll into a tight ball, and hold between your hands right in front of your spectator's nose. Suddenly you clap your hands, and show them absolutely empty. The handkerchief has completely disappeared, right beneath his very eyes!

The closeness of the trick is what makes it possible. The advantage is not with the spectator, but with you. When you are holding the handkerchief right in front of his face, take hold of it with the right hand, and raising your hands slightly, just above his eyes, slap your right wrist against your left hand. The palm of the right hand is directly towards the spectator, and thus you project the handkerchief over his head so suddenly and so rapidly that he does not catch sight of it. Then you clap your hands and show them empty.

If possible, throw the handkerchief so that it falls behind a chair or a table.

10. THE FADEAWAY KNOT TRICK

This is a very pretty disappearing knot trick.

Hold the handkerchief by corners diagonally opposite, between

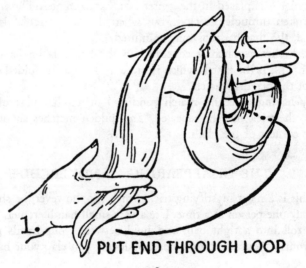

1. PUT END THROUGH LOOP

the second fingers and forefingers of both hands. The right hand, starting from the body, loops the center of the handkerchief over the left thumb. Then the right hand pushes the right end of the handkerchief under the left end of the handkerchief, from the outer side, in towards the body.

The center of the handkerchief is pressed firmly against the upraised knee, and the hands pull the ends downwards. As a result, the center of the handkerchief tightens on the knee into what appears to be a genuine knot; but that is due entirely to the pressure of the knee. When the ends are jerked suddenly, the tight "knot" dissolves in an instant.

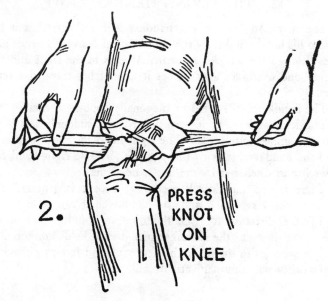

2. PRESS KNOT ON KNEE

11. THE HYPNOTIZED HANDKERCHIEF

The magician takes a folded handkerchief from his pocket—a neat handkerchief which has been ironed. He spreads it upon the table, and grasping the center, raises it slowly upward. When he has the handkerchief almost standing, he removes his hand, makes a mystic pass, and there the handkerchief remains.

The obvious conclusion is that something is supporting it; but the magician lifts the handkerchief, spreads it out, and shows that it contains nothing.

As a matter of fact, nothing is necessary to make the handkerchief stand in this peculiar position. It does so of its own accord, due to the creases, which support its slight weight.

12. THE FLYING HANDKERCHIEF

The magician takes a silk handkerchief and stretches it between his hands. Suddenly the handkerchief leaves his hands and flies through the air like an arrow. It goes to the right and the right hand overtakes and catches it after it has traveled several feet.

The handkerchief is held by diagonally opposite corners.

The left hand draws it very tightly, and suddenly lets it go with an imperceptible snap. The right hand instantly releases it and the handkerchief sails through the air. The right hand follows it and catches it by the left hand corner.

There is a certain knack necessary; once it is acquired, the trick works very easily, and the handkerchief can be made to fly in either direction. It is essential to release both hands at almost the same instant, the handkerchief being held horizontally. People who try to duplicate this feat will find it very difficult—in fact they will almost invariably fail.

13. THE PERFECT DISSOLVING KNOT

There are various methods of making two silk handkerchiefs untie themselves; here is one that is new, effective, and certain.

The two corners of two handkerchiefs are tied in what appears to be a double knot. In fact the knot may be drawn tight by any-one. But when the handkerchiefs are tossed in the air, the knot immediately disappears.

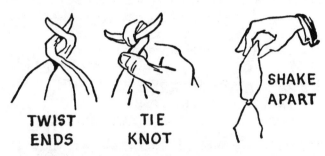

TWIST ENDS **TIE KNOT** **SHAKE APART**

The first knot, made rapidly, is nothing but a twist. The second knot, which seems to make it a double knot, is a simple single knot. The single knot would not hold the handkerchiefs together, but because of the twist, it does hold them, and it can be pulled very tightly, provided that the hands hold the handkerchiefs to keep the twist from coming undone. The twist stops the single knot, and the result is a tight-looking knot that is strong enough to support the lower handkerchief when the upper one is held alone.

When the handkerchiefs are thrown in the air, or shaken, they instantly fall apart.

14. A SUDDEN KNOT

The magician takes a silk handkerchief and lays it across his left thumb, the end going down between the thumb and the palm. He takes the free end of the handkerchief and brings it up under the thumb, then he doubles down the free end, and holds it between the tips of the left thumb and forefinger, making a loop.

Seizing the lower end of the handkerchief with his right hand, he states that he will push it through the loop instantly, with his eyes shut. With a quick motion, he apparently does so, tying the handkerchief into a sudden knot.

END TO GO THROUGH LOOP   CARRY LEFT END OVER THUMB   END THROUGH LOOP

The end of the handkerchief is not pushed through the loop at all. Instead it is quickly swung around the tip of the left thumb and pulled straight back. The left hand must not release the handkerchief at all. A knot is immediately formed upon the left thumb, with a loop that appears to be the one originally there.

This trick is surprisingly easy to perform and is quickly learned when tried.

15. AN ESCAPE

The magician takes a handkerchief and wraps it around his left wrist. He places his right wrist on top, and asks someone to draw the ends of the handkerchief around it, and tie them in a knot. The magician then appears to be tightly bound; but when he turns his back, he instantly escapes.

When the ends of the handkerchief are brought up over the left wrist, the right end should be in front. The right wrist is laid upon the crossing, with the right fingers pointing to the left elbow. Then the ends are brought over the right wrist and are tied.

Everything looks secure; and the hands are held in a stout binding which is shaped exactly like a figure 8.

To release, the magician simply swings his right hand to the right and his left to the left, so that the fingers come together. This untwists the handkerchief and makes an immediate release possible.

A person can get back into this tie as easily as he got out, by reversing the movements. It can be done behind the back, if desired.

16. HANDKERCHIEF ON THE STRING

The wrists are tied with a piece of cord, a length of string extending between them.

The magician shows a handkerchief which is tied so that it forms a loop—two diagonal corners being tied together.

Turning his back for a moment, he passes the handkerchief on the length of string which is between his wrists.

Method: Slide the handkerchief up the arm, drawing it *under* the loop of cord that encircles the left wrist. It will then fall on the string between the wrists. The whole operation takes but a few seconds.

CHAPTER XI

LIQUID TRICKS

Tricks with liquids are always effective; for they are easily seen, and always appear to be difficult. One of the first tricks I ever performed employed liquids, and I will explain it as the first item of this chapter.

1. INK TO WATER

A glass is exhibited, partly filled with ink. The magician dips a playing card in the ink, and brings it out, with its lower half covered with the fluid. Then he covers the glass with a napkin or a large handkerchief. When he removes the cloth, the ink has changed to water!

Method: The interior of the glass is lined with a cylinder of black silk. A piece of black thread, with a small button on the end, is attached to the cylinder. The button dangles over the rim of the glass. When the magician removes the handkerchief he grips the button through the cloth, and thus carries the lining away. The handkerchief may then be rolled up and tossed aside.

The inking of the card is accomplished by having a double-faced card with one side of the card already blackened part way. The card is turned around when it is dipped in the "ink," and the reverse side is shown. If a large glass receptable is used, goldfish may be put in the water and they will be seen swimming there after the transformation.

LIQUID TRICKS

2. WATER TO INK

The change of a glass of water to a glass of ink is accomplished by an entirely different method. In this case, the magician uses an "ink tablet," which is hidden in the folds of the handkerchief. The tablet dissolves quickly in warm water and makes a glass of ink. Tablets that make an imitation ink are sold by dealers in magical apparatus; but more concentrated tablets, used for making real ink, may be purchased at stationery stores.*

3. WATER TO WINE

A glass of water, covered with a handkerchief, may be transformed into a glass of "wine" as easily as into a glass of ink. To do this, obtain a few crystals of potassium permanganate and drop them into the glass when you cover it with a handkerchief. Tilting the glass under the handkerchief helps in the dissolution of the crystals, and a glassful of wine-colored liquid will result.*

4. WINE TO WATER

The instantaneous transformation of wine to water may be effected by merely pouring the liquid from one glass into another. The "wine" is water in which potassium permanganate has been dissolved. The other glass contains a small quantity of hydrogen peroxide, which, being colorless, is not observed. As soon as the "wine" is poured into the "empty" glass, it changes to "water."*

5. TWO GOBLETS

Take a small goblet about one-third full with water, or some other liquid. Set a second goblet upside down upon the first.

* These liquids are not drinkable.

The trick is to pour the contents of the lower glass into the upper glass, without touching the upper glass with your hand, and without anyone else touching the upper glass. To make the problem still more difficult, the upper glass cannot be set on the table or on the floor until it has had the liquid poured into it!

It sounds impossible, but it can be done.

Bend your head well forward, so that you can grip the further side of the foot of the upper goblet between your teeth. Then bend your head well backwards, and you will be holding the goblet firmly in an upright position. Pick up the lower goblet and pour its contents into the goblet you are holding in your mouth.

Be careful not to use too much liquid; the weight of it is something of a factor, as well as the difficulty in pouring.

6. WINE AND WATER (WITHOUT CHEMICALS)

The magician has a glass of wine, standing on a box. He covers it with a handkerchief, and when the cloth is removed, a green crème de menthe has replaced the wine. The handkerchief again covers the glass, and this time water is the resulting liquid. The water is drinkable.

A small goblet should be used. Obtain two pieces of transparent celluloid; one red, the other green, and cut them to fit the goblet. Fill the goblet with water, insert the flat pieces of celluloid, and from two feet away, the glass will appear to contain wine. The refraction of the water makes the illusion perfect.

When the handkerchief is first drawn over the glass, remove the red celluloid and drop it behind the box. Then show the glass. The next time, take away the green celluloid, and drop it along with the other.

If desired the green may be taken away first, leaving claret instead of crème de menthe. A yellow or amber colored celluloid may also be added; it will not affect the colors of the others, but if it is left to the last, it will produce another liquid.

7. THE DRY BOWL

Pour some water into a shallow bowl, then drop two or three coins into the water. The trick is to remove the coins without wetting the fingers. The bowl must not be removed from its present position. In fact, so many conditions may be imposed that the trick will seem absolutely impossible.

There is a very ingenious method of accomplishing the desired result. Put some loose paper into a glass, and set fire to the paper. While it is blazing, quickly invert the glass in the center of the bowl. The water will be sucked up into the glass and you can remove the coins.

8. GRAVITY DEFIED

A tumbler is filled with water, and a sheet of paper is placed over the mouth. Then the tumbler is inverted, but the water does not escape. This is a simple problem in physics, and many persons know that it can be accomplished, so not much surprise will be evidenced. But when you deliberately pull the paper from the mouth of the tumbler, and the water still remains there, a real mystery will be created!

When the tumbler is held over a pitcher, or a bowl, the water suddenly leaves the glass and falls into the pitcher.

A stout disc of transparent celluloid is required for this trick; and the glass used should have a rather flat edge. The celluloid is lying on the table, under the piece of paper (which should be slightly moistened).

When the glass is filled with water, the paper is laid over its mouth, and the celluloid is thus adjusted to the tumbler. When the glass is inverted, the water does not escape. The hand should be pressed against the paper during the inversion.

When the paper is removed, the transparent celluloid is invisible, and the water alone appears to occupy the glass. At the proper moment, touch the projecting edge of the disc with the tip of your finger, and water and disc will drop into the pitcher.

The glass may be specially prepared for this experiment, by having a tiny hole bored in the side of the bottom. In this case, a finger is kept over the air-hole until the last instant. When the finger is removed, the inrushing air will release the disc and finish the trick automatically.

9. THE DRY HAND

The magician dips his hand into a bowl of water. When he removes the hand, it is still dry!

This is due to a preparation applied to the hand. Talcum and lycopodium powders have been recommended, but neither is entirely satisfactory. The best substance is stearate of zinc. If this powder is thoroughly rubbed into the hand, its presence will not be detected; yet when the hand is thrust into the water, and instantly removed, it will be quite dry.

10. DISAPPEARING WATER

This is a trick of pseudo-spiritistic nature. A glass of water is covered with paper strips, so that no one can drink from it. The lights are turned out, and the performer's hands are held. When the lights come on again, the water is gone!

The magician has a drinking straw in his inside coat pocket. He reaches with his mouth, obtains the straw and drinks the water. Then he drops the straw back in his pocket, and calls for the lights.

LIQUID TRICKS

11. GLASS OF WATER FROM POCKET

The production of a glass, filled with water, from the pocket, never fails to create amazement; yet the explanation is very simple.

The glass is covered with a cap of sheet rubber. Special caps are manufactured for this purpose; if they are not obtainable, a sheet of rubber, such as one cut from a toy balloon, will fill the bill. In this case, a heavy rubber band should be used to hold the rubber cover in place.

In performing the trick, grip the glass through the coat with one hand, and hold it upright. With the other hand, reach in, peel off the cover and produce the glass in a nonchalant manner.

12. THE WHIRLING GLASS

This is a feat of dexterity that appears to be very difficult. The magician picks up a glass and swings it around in the air, turning it upside down, and finally bringing it right side up without spilling a drop of the liquid in the glass, which may be about three-quarters full.

The trick should first be practised out of doors or over a bathtub. The glass is held flat on the palm of the hand. Then the arm is held stiff, and is swung in a semicircle, ending with the glass held in a backhand position. Once the knack is acquired, the trick may be performed with impunity, as the centrifugal force keeps the liquid from falling out. People who attempt to duplicate the feat seldom succeed as their nerve fails them and they unconsciously twist the wrist instead of holding the arm stiff.

There is a certain type of trick glass, sold by novelty stores that can be used in this experiment. The glass is made like a goblet, but there is a layer of glass at the mouth, so that no liquid may be poured in or out. The stem, however, is hollow, and the glass is filled through the stem, a small cork keeping the liquid in. If the goblet is filled with milk or grape juice, it has all the appearance of a normal glass; to add to the illusion, a little of the liquid may be poured on top of the glass, which is concave. Pretending that the glass is too full, the magician pours out the little liquid that is on top, thus making the glass appear quite ordinary. He may then whirl the glass in the air, and catch it without spilling a drop. He should, of course, remove the glass before anyone happens to examine it closely.

CHAPTER XII

MATCH-BOX TRICKS

1. THE VANISHING MATCHES

A box is shown full of matches, and is laid on the table. After a time the magician picks it up, and shakes it so the matches rattle.

"Plenty of matches there," he remarks. "Take one out." Someone opens the box. It is empty!

Before performing the trick the magician substitutes an empty box for the full one. Up his sleeve he has a partly filled box of matches (preferably a half size box). When he shakes the empty box, the audience hears the sound of the matches in the hidden box and supposes the visible box is still full of matches.

2. MONTE WITH MATCHES

A trick that rivals the famous "Three Card Monte" may be performed with *match-boxes*. Three boxes are used one of which contains matches. The magician mixes them around on the table and asks someone to pick up the full box. Somehow or other, the spectator always gets an empty box.

This is due to an application of the method used in the preceding trick. A full box, held in place, up the magician's sleeve, by a rubber band, makes one of the empty boxes appear to be full when the magician shakes it. The spectators follow the box in which they hear the matches rattle. The trick can be worked with three empty boxes; but the audience supposes one is full, and the magician keeps up the delusion by occasionally shaking a box.

3. CUTTING THROUGH A MATCH-BOX

This is an up to date novelty in match tricks. A *match-box* is shown with a crosswise slit in the middle of the top and the sides. The magician opens the box slightly, showing the heads of the matches; then he closes it and pushes a playing card down into the slit. To the surprise of everyone the card apparently cuts right through the matches to the bottom of the box. Then the magician pushes the drawer of the box back and forth, showing the heads at one end and the blanks at the other!

Method: The drawer of the box is previously divided into three sections, crosswise and the sides of the middle section are cut away. The end sections are provided with little blocks of paper or cardboard, which are glued in place, and on top of these are glued the ends of matches, heads at one end, blanks at the other. Thus if the drawer is opened slightly, it appears to be full of matches.

The card is inserted slowly as though cutting through a box full of matches. Then the drawer may be pushed back and forth, showing matches at both ends. The card stops the progress of the drawer, so there is no danger of revealing the hollow center.

The box should be pocketed with the card still through it; or the card may be withdrawn and tossed for examination while the box is pocketed. A duplicate (unprepared) box can be kept in the pocket to be brought out later on.

4. APPEARING MATCHES

A *match-box* is shown with the drawer half opened. The box is empty. The drawer is closed and when it is reopened, a number of matches are within.

The matches are in the box all the time but they are wedged between the end of the drawer and the inside of the cover. Thus the box may be shown apparently empty. When the drawer is closed, (the fingers being held at the end to prevent the matches from pushing out), the matches will fall in the drawer.

A whole layer of matches may be produced in this manner. Some match-boxes are sold which are only half the height of the usual match-box. They are especially suited for this trick, as the layer of matches makes a greater showing.

5. MATCHES THROUGH THE TABLE

This is a very surprising trick with matches, and one that is quite new. A box of matches is stood on end, on the table, the drawer being part way open, showing the box filled with matches.

Holding the box with his left hand, the magician strikes the open drawer with his right hand and drives it shut. Then he reaches under the table with the left hand and brings up all the matches. The drawer is opened, and found to be quite empty.

For this trick you require a little contrivance which can be made very easily. Cut about one third off the end of a drawer of a match box. Cut a number of matches to the same size, and glue them in the portion of the drawer.

Then take an empty match-box, and stick the imitation drawer on the end. To all appearances you have a full box of matches, which is pushed part way open. Stand the box on the table; hold it with the left hand. Then strike the imitation drawer with the right hand, and carry it away in the bend of the fingers. The spectators see the end of the genuine drawer, and think you have merely driven the box shut.

Reach under the table, and bring up a lot of loose matches, which you have concealed there. Then let the people examine the empty box while you quietly pocket the imitation drawer.

6. THE ADHESIVE MATCH–BOX

This is an interesting little item in connection with match tricks. Taking a box of matches, you set it against your coat sleeve and it sticks there. The box may be examined.

Use a box of blue-tipped matches, which has sandpaper on the sides. Place the side of the box against the sleeve and it will adhere there.

7. THE DIMINISHING MATCH–BOX

The following trick requires a slight amount of skill, but it is worth the practice. You have a half-opened box of matches, which is filled. The left hand is closed in a fist, and the box is held in the end of the fist. The right hand shuts the drawer of the box and pushes the box into the left fist. But when the left fist is opened, the match-box is only one-half its original size!

All you need is an ordinary match box and a half-size box such as can be purchased at many novelty or cigar stores. The large box should be tightly filled with matches so that they will not rattle when the box is closed, but the small box is not quite full.

Push the drawer of the large box nearly open and you will find a large hiding place inside the cover where you can conceal the small box. Of course the protruding drawer of the large box is towards the audience. Then you are ready for business.

Show the box, and grip the inner end in your left fist, by the thumb. Turn your right side towards your audience. Now the right hand is placed squarely over the protruding drawer, and it pushes the drawer shut, thus ejecting the small box into the left fist. The right hand firmly grips the large box and carries it away, the box being hidden in the closed right hand.

At the same instant, the left hand is raised, the eyes follow it, and it is shaken slightly. The spectators hear the matches rattle, and they catch a glimpse of the box in the left fist, so they think the large box has been pushed in there. If the magician is seated at a table, he should lower his right hand and let the large box fall in his lap. If he is standing, he should immediately turn his left side towards the audience, while shaking the little box and then throw the box on the table, while the right hand pockets the large box.

8. RIBBON FROM THE MATCH

The magician takes a box of matches, after showing his hands empty. He removes a match and strikes it, and then produces a long coil of ribbon from the lighted match.

To do this, push the drawer of the match-box halfway open and insert the coiled-up ribbon in back of the drawer. The match-box is laid on the table with the open end towards the audience.

The hands are shown empty. The left hand picks up the box, while the right hand extracts the match. The drawer of the box is then pushed shut—a most natural procedure—which ejects the ribbon into the left hand. The right hand lights the match, and the left approaches, extinguishes the match and pretends to draw the ribbon from the smoke.

CHAPTER XIII

MATCH TRICKS

1. FOUR TRIANGLES

This is more of a puzzle than a trick but it is so perplexing that it deserves mention. Six matches are laid on the table, to be made into four triangles. All the triangles must be the same size

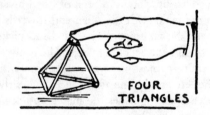

FOUR
TRIANGLES

and the matches must not be broken or crossed.

The solution is to lay three matches in the form of a triangle and set the other three so they form a tripod, each leg starting from an apex of the triangle. Thus four perfect triangles are formed, but only one is on the horizontal plane.

2. PENETRATING MATCHES

Each hand holds a match, by the ends, between the thumb and forefinger. The hands are brought together, and the matches apparently pass through one another, becoming linked. They are drawn apart, and pushed back and forth.

MATCH TRICKS

Use sulphur matches for this trick. Moisten the tip of the right forefinger, and when it is pressed against the head of one match, the match will stick to it. When the hands are brought together, the right forefinger is raised for an instant; the match comes up with it, and permits the passage of the left hand match. The matches are drawn apart in the same manner. The hands should be kept in continuous motion during the "penetration."

3. THE MISSING LIGHT

When a person wants a lighted match, try this little trick. You light a match and hold it out to him. Of course he takes the unlighted end. So you walk away, carrying the light, while he has nothing but the stump of a match.

The match is previously broken in the center. Hold the two portions together when you light the match. Extend your hand and the person will take the broken end while you still have the light.

4. MYSTIC SAFETY MATCHES

Safety matches can only be struck on the box. Everyone knows that. Therefore they will be surprised to see you blissfully light a safety match on the sole of your shoe!

This requires a little previous preparation. Take a match box and rub the side of it against the sole of your shoe, at the instep. Enough of the striking substance will be transferred so that you can light a match on your shoe.

5. ONE AT A TIME

This is a very pretty trick with matches. Two or three matches are used. The right hand takes them one at a time, and, moving up and down, causes the matches to disappear, the hand being shown empty with the fingers wide apart.

Method: You must wear a finger ring on your third finger. Bend in the third and fourth fingers, while the thumb and first two fingers, which are holding the match, push it down in under the ring, and in back of the finger. The hand is kept in motion, and when the match is in place the fingers are spread wide apart.

6. BALANCING A MATCH

Here is a clever method of balancing a match on the back of the thumb.

Set the bottom of the match upon the knuckle of one thumb and bend the thumb inward. Then extend your thumb and the match will be set in a wrinkle or crease in the skin. By moving the hand slightly it is an easy matter to keep the match in an upright position.

7. BURN–OUT MATCHES

Matches that go out as soon as they are lighted always create considerable amusement. These matches are very easily prepared. Obtain some sodium silicate, which is commonly known as water glass, and paint the matches with it, just below the heads. Only a narrow strip needs to be painted around each match. The matches will light when they are struck, but will go out as soon as the flame encounters the water glass.

8. THE MATCH SQUARE

This is a puzzle with matches; but it is so novel that it is quite as interesting as the average match trick.

Lay four matches in the form of a cross, as illustrated in Fig. 1. The problem is to move one match and make the matches form the sides of a perfect square.

Solution: Move one match about a sixteenth of an inch, as shown in Fig. 2. Thus the matches will form the sides of a

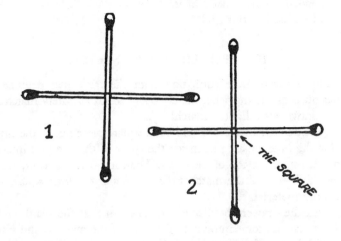

square, but it will be a very tiny square indeed! Nevertheless it fulfills the conditions of the problem to the letter.

9. LIGHTED MATCH FROM POCKET

Taking a lighted match from the pocket is a very surprising little trick. All that is necessary is to have an empty box of safety matches in the pocket, with a loose match lying beside it. In taking the match from your pocket, strike it on the box by merely sliding it out. There is no danger from the match as it comes clear of the pocket just as the flame breaks forth.

A more elaborate trick is the "Lighted Candle From Pocket," which is performed in the same way. The candle is in the inside coat pocket, and instead of the wick it has a blue-tipped match in its end. While the right hand presses the outside of the pocket and holds the match-box steady, the left hand reaches in, obtains the candle and strikes it on the box, immediately bringing it from the pocket.

Wooden candles, made in imitation of the usual wax candle, are often used in this trick.

10. SELF–LIGHTING MATCH

This is even more surprising than the trick just described, inasmuch as the magician merely opens a box of safety matches, and draws out a lighted match!

Take another match box and cut a square piece out of the side. Glue the little square just inside the cover of the box you intend to use, under the top of the cover. Then insert the drawer, with the blank ends of the matches directly under the little square of striking material.

Push the drawer about one-third open so that the blank ends of the matches come into view. Take one of the matches and start to withdraw it from the box. In so doing, "lever" the match on the end of the drawer, and press downward so that the head of the match is drawn against the hidden square of striking material. The match will burst into flame just as you draw it from the box.

11. THE MULTIPLYING MATCH

The magician holds a blue-tipped match between the thumb and forefinger of his right hand. There is nothing else in either hand. The hands are brought together and the match immediately is joined by another match so that each hand holds a single match.

Only one match is used, but it is previously prepared. Take a sharp knife or a razor blade and split the match down the center, head and all. Press the two halves carefully together, holding them at the center, and they can be exhibited as a single match.

When the hands are brought together, each hand takes a section of the match, and, while the hands are waving up and down, the matches are turned so that the flat sides are away from the audience. The matches should be held at the base, one between the thumb and forefinger of each hand. The spectators can see only one side of each section, and from two feet away, the halves look like perfect matches.

If the match has been carefully split, each half may be lighted.

12. THE STANDING MATCH

Making a match stand upright on the surface of a wooden table seems to be a feat of very careful balancing. Anyone who tries it will give it up as impossible, but you can do it with very little difficulty.

There is a trick to it. Secretly moisten the tips of your left thumb and forefinger. After various persons have been unable to make the match stand, take it (by the bottom) between your left thumb and forefinger, thus moistening the end of the match. Transfer the match to your right hand and you can make it stand upright by simply pressing it against the table.

13. SHOOTING THE MATCH

A match is lighted, and another match is placed head to head with it. The instant the second match is ignited, the magician blows out both matches.

Then he sets one match upright in the drawer of the match-box, using the drawer to wedge it in place.

He sets another match on his left hand and flicks it with his right. It flies through the air and knocks off the uppermost of the two matches.

The secret of this bit of markmanship is to aim the match straight for the target; then flick it so that it revolves while going through the air. With a little practice a direct hit will be scored nearly every time.

14. SIX AND ELEVEN

Place six matches so that they form the Roman number 11, namely XI.

State that in Rome, half of eleven was supposed to be six; so half of the number will be six.

To prove this, take away half of the matches—the lower half. The figure X is formed by four matches, and I is formed by two. Taking away the lower half leaves VI, the Roman number for 6.

15. RED AND BLUE

A red-tipped match is shown and is placed in the left hand. When the hand is opened, the tip of the match is blue.

With a bit of wax attach a red tip to the bottom of a blue-tipped match. Hold the blue tip between your right thumb and forefinger, and exhibit the match as a red-tipped one.

Lay the match in the left hand. Turn the hand over, and pretend to push the match further in. This enables you to grip the red tip between the thumb and forefinger, and to draw it from the hand.

Open the hand and show the blue-tipped match, which may be examined.

16. APPEARING PAPER MATCHES

The magician opens a package of paper matches.

He tears out all of the paper matches and drops them in his pocket, immediately closing the package.

When the package is reopened, the matches are back again!

This is a very clever trick. The package of paper matches has four layers. Separate the front two from the rear two, leaving a slight gap. Open the package and pretend to tuck back the flap, but really slide it in between the front and rear layers.

This is done as you are about to show the matches. You then apparently show all the matches; but the cover hides half of them. Tear off the matches that are in view and pocket them. Slide the flap over the stumps and lay the package on the table. When you open it, it appears to be filled with matches again.

17. CROSS TO SQUARE

Two matches are held in the form of a cross, the thumb and forefinger hiding the join.

The magician says that he can form a square with those two matches—using them just as they are, without breaking them.

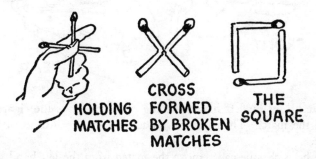

HOLDING MATCHES

CROSS FORMED BY BROKEN MATCHES

THE SQUARE

When he lays the matches on the table the trick is done. The matches have been broken beforehand so that each one forms a right angle, but the matches are not completely broken.

What looks like a cross of two matches, when held in the hand, is really the two right angled matches. When they are laid on the table, each one is two sided, and the formation of the square is easy.

18. MATCH TO CIGARETTE

The magician holds a match in his right hand. He pushes it through his left hand and a cigarette comes out instead of the match.

The match is held between the right thumb and forefinger in an upright position. This enables the magician to conceal the cigarette in back of his thumb and second finger. (See Figs. 1 and 2.)

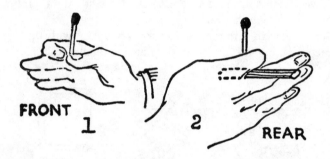

He brings his left hand over the right and grips the cigarette and the match. Then he draws out the cigarette instead of the match.

If he wishes he can remove the match from the left hand and push it up into the fist with the right hand. In doing this he pushes the match *into the cigarette*, which has previously been relieved of some of its contents.

CHAPTER XIV

MISCELLANEOUS TRICKS

1. THE JUMPING RULER

A ruler is pushed down into the closed fist. At the word "Go," the ruler jumps up to the ceiling.

Method: Slip a rubber band over the second finger of the hand. Close the fist with the thumb in front and the elastic will not be seen. Push the ruler down into the fist so that it engages the rubber band, but clench the ruler firmly. As soon as you release pressure the ruler will jump out of the hand. The rubber band may be dropped on the floor.

2. CHANGING SPOOLS

Two spools, one containing black silk thread, the other red, are threaded on a string, and the ends are held. A handkerchief is thrown over the spools and the magician reaches beneath it. When he removes the handkerchief, the spools have changed their positions. The red, which was originally on the right, is now on the left.

To perform this trick, obtain two strips of paper which match the thread on the spools. Cover the black thread with red paper, gluing it to form a tight cylinder; and cover the red thread with black paper. The spools will appear quite ordinary. When they are under the cloth, tear the paper coverings off the spools, and remove the papers with the handkerchief. Thus the spools will apparently be transposed. Both the spools and the string may be thoroughly examined at the conclusion of the trick.

3. THE FLOWER IN THE BUTTONHOLE

The Flower in the Buttonhole is a very pretty little trick that has been performed by a number of professional magicians. The effect is very quick and surprising. The magician points to his empty buttonhole; waves his right hand over it, and a flower appears there instantly.

An artificial flower is used, preferably a rose. A piece of black cord elastic is attached to the stem, and it runs through the buttonhole, under the lapel and down to a lower buttonhole, where it is pulled taut and firmly looped. The flower is placed under the left armpit, stretching the cord elastic across from the buttonhole. As the right hand is passed over the buttonhole, the left arm is lifted slightly, and the flower makes its instant appearance.

4. THE THREE BEADS

Three beads are threaded on a wire ring, the ends of which are twisted so firmly that it would be impossible to remove the beads very quickly.

In color, the beads are red, white and blue.

The magician states that he will mysteriously arrange the colors in any order: red, blue, white; white, red, blue—any order the audience may choose.

An order is decided upon and the magician puts the ring behind his back. When he draws it forth, the beads are arranged in their chosen order!

This trick is simple but effective. Most people will not realize it, but it is an easy matter to arrange the beads in any desired order by merely running one around the ring.

Red, blue and white is the same as *white, blue, and red,* according to which side the magician counts from. *Red, white and blue* is *blue, white and red;* and *blue, red and white* is *white, red and blue.*

5. A DIFFICULT JOB

Tell a person to stand with his back against a wall. Then lay a dollar bill at his feet, and challenge him to lean forward and pick up the money without bending his knees or moving his feet.

This he will be unable to do, unless he loses his balance. Then he will be unable to return to the standing position. You can offer the dollar bill as a reward, and you will not lose it!

6. THE MYSTIC PROPELLOR

The "Mystic Propellor" is a little wooden propellor attached to the end of a short stick. The propellor is held by a simple pin in the center, and the stick has notches in the top.

When the magician rubs the pencil back and forth along the stick, the propellor revolves rapidly as though controlled by an unseen force.

In rubbing the top of the stick, the magician lets his thumb press against the side. This imparts an imperceptible rotary motion to the stick and that causes the propellor to revolve.

7. PIN THROUGH THE HEAD

This is a surprising little trick with an ordinary pin. The pin is held between the thumb and forefinger, and it is tapped against the forehead, the fingers immediately spreading apart.

The hand goes to the back of the head, and reappears with the pin between the thumb and forefinger.

The pin is attached to the tip of the forefinger by a bit of adhesive tape at the center of the pin. When the fingers press against the forehead, the pin is flat, and remains attached to the finger when it goes to the back of the head. Quick motions are necessary to make this trick effective.

8. PIN THROUGH FINGER

A large safety pin is used in this trick. The magician shows the pin closed, and one bar of it apparently passes through his finger. But he removes the pin and shows the finger uninjured.

The pin is prepared. The point is firmly wedged or soldered to the clasp, and one bar is cut at the center, so that a section is removed. This is slipped over the finger to the center, and it looks as though the pin penetrates the finger.

9. THE TURNOVER KEY

The magician lays a key on his outstretched hand. At his command the key turns over.

Method: The key is placed so that the handle is over the side of the hand. It is set on balance, so that it is ready to topple the moment the hand is tilted. By raising the fingers slightly, the key is made to revolve, with no apparent motion of the hand. An ordinary door key should be used.

10. THE VANISHING CANDLE

A candle is lighted, extinguished, and wrapped in a sheet of paper. The paper is torn in half, and in place of the candle, a hand-kerchief is found.

The candle is an imitation. It is made of a sheet of glazed paper, rolled into a tube, with the tip of a real candle in one end. Thus the candle may be lighted.

The handkerchief is inside the candle. The candle is torn up with the paper and the handkerchief is produced. Confetti or ibbon may be used in place of the handkerchief.

11. THE RUBBER CUBE

A cube of red sponge rubber is used in this clever mystery. It is shown to the spectators; then the magician rubs it between his hands, and when he separates them, there is a rubber cube in each hand!

The cube is nearly two inches square. It is made from a rubber sponge. Cut a slit in the side, and with a pair of small scissors, hollow out the interior of the cube.

Thus the cube becomes a mere shell, but being made of sponge rubber, the opening will be unnoticed.

Another cube, a trifle smaller than the first, is pushed into the first cube. It compresses to a very small size, and the cube within the cube can be safely shown as one.

When the cube is rolled between the hands, the inner cube is forced out, and a cube appears in each hand.

CHAPTER XV

NUMBER TRICKS

This chapter is a short one, dealing with some interesting experiments in numbers. All that is needed is a pencil and paper. The figures will do the rest.

These tricks are well suited to the beginner in magic, as they require no skill whatever.

1. TOTALLING TWENTY

Tell a person to write down five odd figures in a column and add them up to total twenty.

As twenty is an even number, people who try it will soon give it up. But the magician can do it!

Here is the method: Put down 13, 5, 1, and 1. Add these numbers and the total will be 20. But there are only *four* odd numbers. That is true, but there are *five odd figures:* 1, 3, 5, 1, and 1.

The conditions of the trick call for five odd *figures,* which most people take to mean five odd *numbers.*

2. TELLING THE TOTAL

Let a person write down a row of six figures. Then write something on a piece of paper and lay it aside.

Another person writes six figures beneath the first row. Then you write a number of six figures. Another person obliges with a number of six figures, and you do the same. When the sum is added, a total is reached. Your paper is unfolded, and there is the answer!

Method: Note the first number written. Add to it 2,000,000, and subtract 2. That is what you write on the piece of paper. Just put down 2 less than the number written, and put a figure 2 in front of it!

When the second number is written, you write your number. Just add enough to each number in the second row to make each figure total 9.

When the fourth row is written, you write the fifth, and make the fourth row total 9 for every figure. That will bring your answer.

Example: A person writes 347,628. On your paper write 2,347,626.

Now the addition may appear like this:

First row	347,628
Second row	312,799
Your row	687,200
Fourth row	810,204
Your row	189,795
	———————
Total	2,347,626

3. NINE FIGURES

Write something on a piece of paper and lay it aside.

Then write the figures: 1, 2, 3, 4, 5, 6, 7, 8, 9.

Tell a person to cross out a figure. Then you eliminate figures by having them crossed out. When only one is left, open the paper, and there will be the figure!

Method: On the paper write 5. Most persons will cross out 5. If they do so, open the paper and show that the number on it is 5!

If they cross out another number state that you have eliminated one figure, leaving two groups of four.

Ask that four figures be chosen. If 5 is among them, have the other four crossed out. If 5 is not among them, cross them out.

Then have two figures chosen. Repeat—if 5 is there, have the others crossed out. If not, cross out the chosen figures.

Ask that one of the two remaining figures be selected. If 5 is picked, cross out the other. If not, cross out the chosen figure.

It is a case of a certain elimination to the figure 5, a ruse that is never detected.

4. THE GRAND TOTAL

Let a person write down the year of his birth and then the year of his marriage, or his first year of school.

Then he must write his age at the end of the present year, and to it the number of years he has been married, or the number of years since he began school.

In the meantime you have written a total on a paper and put it in an envelope. The total of the person's figures will be the same as the total you wrote.

Here is the reason: The sum will always be twice the number of the present year.

Thus, if the trick is done in 1952:

Year of birth	1900
Year of marriage	1925
Age	52
Years since marriage	27
Total	3904

The number 3904 is two times 1952!

5. CROSS THEM OUT

Write the following numbers in a line: 1, 2, 3, 4, 5, 6, 7, 8, 9, 10. The object is to cross out three groups of numbers, starting from

NUMBER TRICKS

the end of the line, and the last number of each group must be odd. This sounds impossible, as the last group must end with 10! But it can be done.

Method: Start from the *right* end. Thus your first group crossed out can end in 7; the second in 3, and the third in 1.

6. THE MAGIC NUMBER

The magician writes a number on a slip of paper and folds the paper. He asks some one to write down a number of three different figures, as: 6 5 1.

The number must then be reversed, and the smaller subtracted from the larger:

$$\begin{array}{r} 651 \\ -156 \\ \hline 495 \end{array}$$

The result (495) must be reversed and added, thus:

$$\begin{array}{r} 495 \\ +594 \\ \hline 1089 \end{array}$$

When the folded paper is opened, it bears the total 1089!

The secret? Simple enough! No matter what figures the person uses, if he follows instructions, the answer will always be 1089! So you have merely to write that number on your folded slip of paper, and then tell the person what to do!

7. THE FAVORITE NUMBER

Write down the number 12345679.

Give a person a pencil and ask him to pick out his favorite

figu.e. Suppose he says 7. Tell him to multiply the number by 63. He does so, and the answer is a row of sevens, thus:

$$
\begin{array}{r}
12345679 \\
\times\ 63 \\
\hline
37037037 \\
74074074 \\
\hline
777777777
\end{array}
$$

The secret is very simple: When a figure is **named by the person**, mentally multiply that figure by 9, and tell the person to multiply the big number by the total. Thus $9 \times 7 = 63$, so 63 produces the row of sevens. If three was named **as the** favorite figure, the multiplier would be 27.

8.   THE THIRTY–ONE TRICK

Tear a sheet of paper into thirty-six slips and on each slip write the numbers from 1 to 6, making six sets in all. Now tell a person that you and he will take turns drawing slips from the pile, adding the numbers as you go along. The object of the game is to bring the total to *exactly* 31 and whichever person accomplishes that will be the winner.

You will always be the winner because there is a trick to the game. This can best be understood by studying a sample game, the numbers in *italics* representing the slips that *you* draw:

3—5—*2*—6—*1*—4—*3*—1—*6* make the total (from your final slip) of *31*.

All you have to do is bring the totals to the following key-numbers: *3, 10, 17, 24* and finally *31*. You start with a *3* and whatever the other player draws, you pick a slip which will make a total of 7 when added to his. Should he draw a 1, you draw a *6*; when he takes 2, you pick *5*—and so on.

NUMBER TRICKS

As the first player, you are sure to win; but in introducing this trick, you can let the other player draw first. Not knowing the secret, he will generally give you a chance to strike one of the key-numbers prior to *31*. After you have won several games, your opponent will want you to draw first, thinking it will be to your disadvantage, whereas actually it will be your clincher.

CHAPTER XVI

OPTICAL TRICKS

This chapter is devoted to tricks and illusions which require no skill, but which deceive the eye and clearly demonstrate that the old saying "Seeing is Believing" is not to be trusted.

1. WHICH IS LARGER?

Cut out two pieces of cardboard exactly the same size and shape as those shown in the accompanying drawing. (Fig.1.)

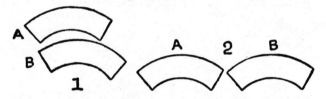

When these are shown to a person—or when you look at them here on the page, it seems certain that the lower one is larger than the upper. In fact no one will doubt the statement if you make it.

However, both figures are exactly the same size. This can be demonstrated by laying one upon the other. (See Fig. 2.)

2. THE COIN IN THE GLASS

Partly fill a glass of water, and place a plate upon it, after you have dropped a dime in the glass.

Then invert the glass and the plate. The water will not come out if you are careful.

Now invite someone to look through the side of the glass. To his surprise he will see two coins; the dime will be apparently above the other, which will appear to be the size of a quarter.

This is a good way to make money!

3. MYSTIC CIRCLES

The circles shown in the drawing are obviously imperfect. No one would accuse them of being true circles, for they are almost egg shaped—at least they appear to be.

But you can safely state that they are perfect circles. This fact

can be demonstrated with the aid of a compass, or by laying coins in the center of the circles. The curving checker-board effect confuses the eyes.

4. A MISSING COIN

Fill a glass of water to the brim, cover it with a small plate, and set it upon a coin.

Then invite people to look into the glass and tell you if there is anything beneath it. As they must look in the side of glass, they will not see the coin, for it will be absolutely invisible.

When you lift the glass and reveal the coin, everyone will wonder where it came from!

5. DRAWING WITH A MIRROR

Show a person a simple diagram of a square with a diagonal cross in the center.

He is supposed to draw this simple diagram; but he must do so with the aid of a mirror, guiding his hand by looking in the glass, while the performer covers his hand so he cannot see it directly.

The person will be unable to draw the diagram. He will go in all sorts of directions, and the result will be very poor.

If the magician is called upon to draw the diagram, he can do so, by one of two methods. First, by practicing beforehand; and second by drawing the diagram by the aid of his hand alone, and paying no attention to what he sees in the mirror.

6. SEEING THROUGH SOLID

There is a very simple method whereby a person can apparently see through a solid object.

All that is required is a tube of paper, about an inch in diameter. The tube is held to the right eye, while the left hand holds the object—a match-box or a playing card, for example—alongside of the tube, on the left.

Both eyes are kept open, and a remarkable illusion results. It appears as though one is looking right through a hole in the center of the object.

7. A GHOST

Here is a way to make a person see a ghost!

Tell him to gaze steadily at the picture shown herewith. He must look at it for about half a minute, under a strong light, keeping his eyes on the tiny cross in the picture.

Then he must turn his gaze toward the wall. As he looks there, a large ghostly image of the picture will appear before his eyes.

Sometimes the image is very clear, and it is often intensified by blinking the eyes a few times.

8. STRANGE LINES

A really remarkable optical illusion is shown here.

It is certain that the border lines of the drawing are straight;

but the two center lines that are as heavy as the borders seem curved.

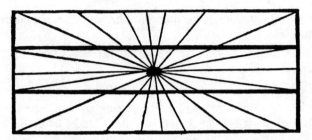

As a matter of fact they are straight, although no one will believe you if you say so. A ruler or the edge of a card, when laid upon the lines, will demonstrate that they are straight.

9. THE SNAKE AND THE BIRD

One of the most amusing of all optical illusions is shown here. The snake is waiting to swallow the bird. To make him do it,

bring the book up close to your eyes, and you will see the bird fly on a bee-line into the snake's mouth.

10.   BOTH SIDES

This is really an optical illusion. The magician states that he will let a person see both sides of a coin at once.

The trick is accomplished by spinning the coin. As its revolutions slow down, both the head and the tail will be plainly seen —apparently at the same time.

CHAPTER XVII

PAPER TRICKS

Many clever little tricks may be performed with pieces of paper. In fact, some of the best experiments in impromptu conjuring are done with paper. One of the most perplexing of all such tricks is called:

1. THE TORN AND RESTORED CIGARETTE PAPER

The magician takes a cigarette paper, and tears it to pieces. He rolls the pieces in a tiny ball, shows his hands empty except for the little ball, and then proceeds to unroll it. The torn paper is restored, and the hands are empty!

A duplicate paper ball is used. It is rolled and concealed between the tips of the first and second fingers of the right hand. All the fingers are bent slightly, and the position of the hand is very natural.

The original paper is torn, rolled into a pellet, and the two pellets are pressed together, so they may be held between the left thumb and forefinger and shown as one, while the hands are shown to be otherwise empty. The paper ball is rolled more tightly, which enables the first and second fingers of the right hand to take away the torn paper pellet.

Then the fingers and thumbs of both hands start to unroll the duplicate paper pellet. To assist this action, the tips of the right fingers are raised to the tongue and are slightly moistened. The torn bits of paper are left in the mouth, and the restored pellet is completely opened, the hands being shown empty.

2. THE RESTORED PAPER NAPKIN

The effect of this trick is similar to the last. A paper napkin or a large square of tissue paper is used, and the magician apparently shows how the trick is done, yet finishes by mystifying his audience.

Three napkins are used. One is rolled in a ball and is placed inside the other two which are formed in a loose cylinder. The magician unrolls the cylinder, and secretly grips the rolled up napkin in the bend of his right fingers.

Then he exhibits the two loose napkins, and rolling one into a ball, shows how it may be concealed under the left fingers. He tears the unrolled napkin, rolls it into a ball, and adds the napkin from the right hand. He holds the two balls as one at the tips of his left fingers, calling attention to the ball that is under the left fingers.

"Now," remarks the magician, "I will exchange the torn pieces for the restored napkin." The right hand approaches, and squeezes the double ball, removing the ball of torn pieces, leaving a restored ball at the tip of the left fingers and thumb, and another restored ball under the left fingers. One restored ball is exchanged for the other, in plain view; and the ball that was under the left fingers is unrolled, and held up to view. It is carelessly rolled into a ball, with the torn pieces from the right hand going inside it, and it is dropped in the pocket by the right hand.

"Here," says the magician, pointing to his left hand, "I still have the torn pieces. Of course it is necessary to dispose of them in some way. Perhaps the best method is to unroll them—and then we find that they have also been mysteriously restored!"

As an additional effect, the magician may have a fourth paper napkin rolled tightly inside the third. When he reaches the denouement of the trick, and shows the torn pieces really restored, he carelessly lets the fourth napkin fall to the floor, where he quickly puts his foot on it. Of course everyone wants to see the little paper ball that is beneath his foot; so after feigning embarrassment the magician picks it up and calmly unrolls it.

3. THE CELEBRITY TRICK

The magician takes a cigarette paper and lays it on the table. He asks some one to name a famous celebrity, now deceased. Suppose Washington is named.

The magician asks some one to carefully roll the paper into a tiny ball. He takes the little pellet, and holding it between the tips of his left thumb and forefinger, places it on the back of the spectator's hand. A few moments later, the paper is unrolled, and the name 'Washington' appears written on it!

This pseudo-psychic mystery is quite astonishing. Yet it is not a difficult trick to perform.

Place a tablet of cigarette papers and a very short pencil in your right trousers pocket, or in the coat pocket. As soon as the celebrity is named, put your hand in the pocket and write the name on the top sheet of paper; then roll up the slip of paper and hold it between the tips of your forefinger and second finger (as with the restored cigarette paper). When you take the pellet rolled by the spectator, bring the hands together and add your pellet, holding the two as one; then, in dropping the pellet on the spectator's hand, retain the spectator's paper with the fingers of your right hand, and drop the pellet that bears the message. The right hand easily disposes of the spectator's pellet, and the trick is virtually completed. You should be careful to perform this trick in a very impressive manner.

4. THE TOUGH NAPKIN

A paper napkin is twisted in rope fashion, and a person is invited to tear it in half by pulling on the ends. The paper will prove too tough to tear. But when others have failed, you take the twisted napkin, and tear it with ease.

To accomplish this, dip your fingers in a glass of water while the other persons are trying to break the napkin. Twist the paper tighter with your fingers, and in so doing, moisten the center. The napkin will then break when you pull the ends.

5.   THE PAPER BRIDGE

Take a sheet of note paper and stretch it between two glasses, so that it forms a sort of bridge. Ask anyone to set another glass on the bridge; the paper will not support the additional weight. The trick is to make the paper bear that weight.

PAPER
PLEATED

The solution of the problem is quite artful: pleat the paper lengthways; then it will bear the weight of the third glass.

6.   THE MARKED PAPER

Take a packet of cigarette papers, and let a person write on one of them, very lightly, so that the paper is not indented. The papers are mixed; then you hold them behind your back, and instantly draw out the marked paper!

Method: Cigarette papers are cut on the bias. You have merely to turn the marked paper around, before it is inserted with the others; and when you hold the packet behind your back, you will discover projecting corners that belong to the marked paper.

7. THREE PAPER SLIPS

Take a small sheet of paper and fold it crosswise into three slips of equal size. Tell a person to write three names on the paper, one in each section, with his own name in the center. He then tears the paper along the creases, and folds each slip in quarters. The paper slips are dropped in a hat, and you immediately reach in without looking and bring out the slip which bears the person's name.

Method: Both edges of the desired slip will be rough. The other slips will each have one smooth edge. Feel for the paper with the rough edges.

8. TRAVELING TISSUE PAPER

The requirements for this trick are two match-boxes and two sheets of tissue paper, one red, the other blue.

Crumple the blue paper and put it in a match-box. Mark the end of the drawer with a blue pencil, and close the box. Crumple the red sheet and put it in the other box, marking the end of the drawer with a red pencil. Thus the marks tell the color of the paper contained in each box.

The two boxes are laid on the table. Pass your hand over them, and open them. In the box with the *red* mark, you find the *blue* paper; while the *red* paper has mysteriously passed to the box with the *blue* mark!

On the reverse end of one drawer you must previously make a red mark, and a blue mark on the reverse end of the other drawer. As each drawer is part way open, these marks will not be seen. Put the red paper in the box which has the hidden blue mark; and

PAPER TRICKS

put the blue paper in the box which bears the concealed red mark. Then mark the front end of each drawer with a color corresponding to the paper that is in the box.

Close the drawers and put the two boxes together. In stepping to the table, or moving some object out of the way, turn the boxes around, so that when you lay them on the table, the red marked box is now blue and the blue is red. Thus when the drawers are opened, the transposition has been effected.

9. THE SHOWER OF PAPER

This is a very pretty trick, of Oriental origin. The magician tears up a piece of tissue paper and soaks the strips in a glass of water. He holds the soaked paper in his left hand, and picking up a fan with the right, fans the wet papers. A flurry of paper flakes immediately emerges from the left hand, and a tiny cloud of paper flies about the magician. The wet paper has disappeared.

Method: Although substitution is required in the trick, no special skill is needed. First cut up some tissue paper into very fine bits, and enclose the flakes in a piece of tissue paper of the same color. A small rubber band will keep the packet closed. Lay the package behind a book, upon which the fan and several sheets of paper are resting.

Pick up a sheet of paper, and lift the packet with it, holding the packet in the left hand, under the fingers. Tear up the sheet of paper, dip it in water, and squeeze it. Bring the hands together and raise the left hand, opening the fingers slightly, so the packet shows through. The audience sees the colored paper and mistakes it for the soaked pieces.

The right hand picks up the fan, and in so doing drops the soaked pieces behind the book. While the right hand fans the left, the left fingers tear open the packet and release the paper shower. After the shower is completed, the right hand closes the fan by striking it against the left; and the left hand takes the fan and

replaces it on the book, dropping the tissue paper covering behind the book.

10. PRODUCTION OF PAPER MONEY

The magician holds a dollar bill in his hands; otherwise his
hands are empty. He pulls up his sleeves, and rubs the dollar bill
between his hands. A dozen more bills appear at his finger tips;
the single dollar has increased into a stack of paper money.

Method: The extra bills are folded lengthways, and are rolled
into a tight cylinder, which is hidden in a fold of the left sleeve,
at the elbow. After the hands are shown empty, the sleeves are
drawn up; and in pulling up the left sleeve, the right hand obtains
the roll of bills, which are then spread out between the hands
under cover of the bill already there.

11. A GENEROUS OFFER

The magician hands a square piece of paper to a person and
tells him that if he can tear it into four equal pieces, the magician
will give him a quarter.

Tearing the paper as required sounds easy enough; so the
person does so, and demands payment. The magician asks to look
at the four slips of paper, and says:

"Yes, you did it. Here's your quarter."

Thereupon he gives the person one of the four pieces of paper,
which is a quarter—of the sheet of paper!

This can be varied by using a slang expression, and offering to
donate "two bits". In this case, two of the pieces of paper are
given, as they represent the two bits mentioned.

12. BLOW THEM AWAY

Three pieces of paper are laid on the back of the hand. The
magician states that he will blow away one, two, or three, as

required, the audience specifying the pieces to be blown away. But the others will not leave the hand.

It seems impossible to blow away two pieces without disturbing the third—or one without blowing the other two also. But the magician accomplishes the feat by placing the fingers of the other hand upon the papers designated to remain. Then when he blows, only the loose paper will fly away.

13. A PAPER TEARING TRICK

There are some very clever methods of tearing and restoring a sheet of tissue paper. This one, however, is new and different.

The magician shows two pieces of tissue paper; one white, the other black. He tears both together and folds them into a small packet. When he unfolds the papers, they are restored—but in the form of a large white square with a square black center.

No trace of the torn sheets remains.

The restored paper is formed beforehand by pasting a black square on each side of the large white one. On one side, the black square is pasted around the edges, and one edge is left open.

The restored paper is then folded into a small package, with the opening on the outside, and it is laid behind an object on a table.

Two ordinary sheets—white and black—are shown. They are laid on the table for a moment. When picked up, the restored package is behind them. They are torn into quarters (keeping the restored sheet hidden), and the entire bundle is turned over, bringing the restored piece to the front. Under cover of this, the hands, with a wavy motion, double up the torn pieces together, and then gradually open the restored paper. This affords ample opportunity to poke the torn pieces into the secret pocket. Thus when the restored paper is fully unfolded, it may be shown on both sides, and the hands can be shown absolutely empty.

14. IT LOOKS EASY

Take a sheet of paper, and tear it into thirds, but do not quite tear the end sections loose. The result is a sheet of paper with two parallel slits, making three flaps.

Hand this to a person and tell him to take hold of the end flaps and keep one in each hand. Then he must tear the end flaps from the center portion of the paper.

It looks easy—but it isn't.

When the person tries to do it, he will surely tear away just one of the end flaps, and not both, as the pull is bound to be unevenly distributed.

15. FROM THE ASHES

The magician uses a strip of tissue paper, which he attaches to a wire, and burns in a candle flame. He lets the ashes fall in one empty hand, and showing the other hand empty, rubs the ashes between his hands, and draws forth the piece of paper, restored to its original condition.

A duplicate strip of paper is used. It is pleated, or folded, and is wrapped into a very small bundle, covered with pink or light manila tissue paper. One hand is wearing a finger ring, and the paper bundle is tucked under the ring.

Both hands can be shown apparently empty; at a distance of a few feet, the little packet cannot be seen, especially if the hands are kept in motion.

In rubbing the ashes it is easy to extract the bundle and draw forth the restored strip of paper. The wrapping falls to the floor.

16. PENNY THROUGH PAPER

Take a small square of paper; cut or tear a hole in the center, making the hole slightly less than the size of a penny. Now lay a penny on the paper and state that you can put the coin through the hole without tearing the paper further.

To all appearances, this is impossible, yet the trick is easily accomplished. Fold the paper crosswise in each direction, the creases running through the hole. Lay the penny on the paper and lift the paper, folding it along one crease. This causes the penny to rest edgewise in the hole.

Next, bend the ends of the paper upward to produce a fold along the other crease. This causes the circular hole to stretch to a long oval and the penny will drop through edgewise. The trick can be done with any size coin, but the hole in the paper must be proportionately large. Preliminary experiment will determine the exact size required.

17. OUT OF SIGHT

This is a catch trick that will really puzzle people until you demonstrate it and show how simply it can be accomplished. The finish itself is quite an unusual surprise, but fulfills the seemingly impossible requirements.

Your claim is this: You can take an ordinary sheet of news-paper, lay it on the floor, and have two people stand on the ends of the paper facing each other. Yet they will be unable to see each other or even to touch each other. The paper is not to be torn, but will be set on the floor exactly as is, and will be intact after the trick.

When every one is sure it can't be done, you proceed to do it. Lay the paper through a doorway. Have one person stand on the far end of the paper, then close the door and tell the other person to stand on the near end. Both persons can face the door, hence each is facing the other. But neither person can see the other nor even touch the other, exactly as you stated.

18. THE MAGIC BLOW

The magician rests a book upon the table, and upon it stands another book. Both books are quite heavy, yet he states that he can knock over the top book by the force of his breath!

This sounds impossible, and it would be, if the magician blew directly upon the book. But just before he is ready, he sets both books upon a large paper bag. Then he blows into the paper bag, inflating it, and that upsets the upper book.

19. A PAPER SNAKE

This paper snake is formed from the outer wrapping of drink-ing straws—thin paper which comes in envelope form, and keeps the straws clean.

The paper covering is broken at one end, and then it is slid down the straws, telescoping as it goes along, until it forms a short pleated tube about two inches long.

When the short tube is laid upon a plate, it begins to act in a snake-like fashion, twisting and turning, raising its head, and be-coming very wiggly.

To make the "snake" act in this life-like manner, the magician must first pour a few drops of water on the plate. When the paper tube is set upon a water-drop it begins to absorb water, and immediately comes to life.

20. TRANSPOSED PAPER SLIPS

The magician takes two small pieces of paper, one red and the other blue. He opens two small metal boxes—of the type that contain thumb-tacks—and he places the pieces of blue paper in one and the pieces of red paper in the other.

He covers the boxes for a moment, and when he opens them, he shows that the red and blue papers have changed places.

PAPER TRICKS

The papers do not change—but the colors actually do; therefore the trick is quite effective. In one of the little metal boxes there is placed a very small quantity of vinegar, or some acid; the other contains a little liquid ammonia.

The paper used is litmus paper, which is obtainable at any drug store, where it can be purchased very cheaply. The blue paper is dropped in the box containing the vinegar; the red paper is dropped in with the ammonia. The chemical action of these liquids on the litmus paper causes the red to change to blue and the blue to red instantly.

21. THE PAPER RIBBON TRICK

Many persons have heard of or have seen the trick in which a magician apparently eats a quantity of paper and then produces it in a long ribbon from his mouth.

The trick is not at all difficult to perform. All that is needed is a small coil of paper ribbon, sold at many stationery stores as "throw out coils" for banquets and dances. The magician has a few slips of tissue paper of the same color as the ribbon, and the ribbon is held beneath the tissue paper.

In taking the paper in the mouth, it is easy to introduce the paper coil without detection. The tissue paper is rolled up by the tongue and held at the side of the mouth, while the ribbon is drawn out, starting from the center of the coil. This is a very surprising and amusing trick.

22. THE MESSAGE ON THE CARD

A small card is placed in an envelope. The envelope is sealed and girded with a broad rubber band.

Then some figures are written in a column. Someone is asked to add them up while the magician writes a person's initials on the envelope. He lets the person hold the envelope.

When the total of the figures is added, the person opens the envelope, and takes out the card. There is the answer on it!

The envelope has a small vertical slit in the center of the face—an opening that is almost as wide as the rubber band. The card is put in, and the band is put around the envelope, hiding the hole.

The magician watches the column of figures—which should be single figures, and mentally adds the total. While someone is adding up the total, he puts the initials on the envelope, and this gives him a chance to push the band aside with his left thumb and write the total in small figures on the card.

The person who holds the envelope sees nothing wrong because of the rubber band. As soon as he has removed the card, by tearing the end of the envelope, the magician takes the envelope and carelessly tears it down the center, destroying traces of the opening.

23. WHAT'S ON THE PAPER?

This is an interesting and amusing "catch".

The magician tells a person to write anything he chooses on a piece of paper, and to fold the paper and put it on the floor. To prevent the magician from seeing anything, the person is told to put his foot on the folded paper.

The magician announces that although he cannot see the writing, he can tell exactly what is on the paper, if the person wishes him to do so.

"All right", says the person who wrote the message. "Tell me, what's on the paper?"

"Your foot", replies the magician—and the spectator must admit that the reply is correct!

24. THREE CARDS

The magician shows three plain cards: one red, one white, and one blue. He drops them in a borrowed hat.

Then he takes out the red card and the white card. He puts them in his trousers pocket.

"What is the color of the card in the hat?" he asks.

"Blue!" is the reply.

The hat is turned over, and the *red* card is found in the hat while the blue and white are taken from the pocket!

The supposed blue card used in the trick is blue on one side only. On the other side it is red. But as the magician shows only one side, the audience naturally supposes that they see a red card, a white card, and a blue card.

As soon as the cards are in the hat, the magician turns over the "blue" card, and brings it out so that the red side shows. Then he follows with the white card, carelessly showing both sides.

These cards are placed in the pocket and the red card is found in the hat. In his pocket the magician has a real blue card which he draws out with the white one, and he throws those two cards on the table.

If he wishes, he can push the red and blue card up into the top corner of his pocket and carelessly turn the pocket inside out.

25. PENETRATING PAPER

An envelope is used in this trick—one of the type that opens at the end. Also a piece of stout, colored paper that is nearly as large as the envelope.

The magician pushes the paper into the envelope, and holds the envelope in front of the light to show the paper within. Then, in plain view, he pushes a pencil through the envelope and the paper, and after it a piece of ribbon. But when he pulls out the sheet of paper, it is uninjured!

Method: The envelope has a slit (cut with a sharp knife or safety-razor blade), near the center. When the paper is pushed in it goes through the slit.

The other side of the envelope is held in view and objects are

pushed through by the right hand. The left fingers hold the envelope and they bend back the piece of paper so that it is not
injured. Then the paper can be removed from the envelope and
shown, while the envelope is torn and tossed away, because it is of
no further use. The tear is made at the slit.

26. THE PAPER BAG

This is a trick of paper tearing.

A piece of paper is folded diagonally and diagonally again,
making a triangle. Then it is cut with alternate slits. (See Fig. 1.)

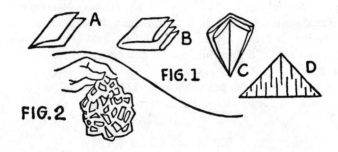

The paper is opened, and turned inside out. The corners are
held and the center is pulled down, the result being an ornamental
mesh-bag. (See Fig. 2.)

27. THE PAPER LADDER

Roll a piece of paper into a tube. Add another piece of paper,
making the ends overlap and continue thus until with several
sheets of large paper a thick tube has been formed.

Tear the paper crossways at the center—half way through. Then
tear a slit down, and a slit up—a distance of a few inches.

Press the paper flat, so the two flaps are at the top. Bend them back, hold the ends and draw out the center of the roll, making a large and ornamental ladder.

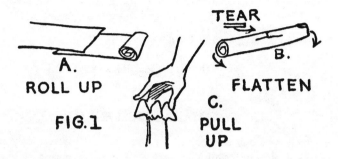

This is shown in the drawing above.

The trick is very effective when several sheets of stout paper are used—all of different colors.

CHAPTER XVIII

PENCIL TRICKS

1. THE MAGNETIC PENCIL

A pencil is held at the magician's finger tips. It mysteriously adheres there, although only two fingers are pressed against it. Then the pencil is given for examination, and the hand is shown to be unprepared.

Method: Take a loop of black thread and pass it through a buttonhole of your coat. Insert the pencil (which should be a dark one), through the loop. Press outwards against the pencil with the backs of your fingers, letting the thread run between the fingers. The pressure will make the pencil stick to the fingers. As soon as pressure is released, the pencil will slip from the loop, which will fall unseen against your coat.

A dark coat should be worn when this trick is performed.

2. THE "VANISHING" PENCIL

A pencil is rolled in a sheet of paper. The paper is immediately torn to pieces, and the pencil is gone!

The pencil is nothing but a hollow paper tube. A glazed, colored paper is the best to use. A real pencil tip is inserted in one end of the tube; and the eraser end of a pencil in the other end. You can write with the pencil and it will appear quite ordinary. But when you roll it up in a sheet of paper, you can tear the paper into several pieces, to prove that the pencil has gone.

PENCIL TRICKS

3. TURNABOUT PENCIL

A pencil is exhibited and is pushed into a paper tube, the point of the pencil going in last. When the pencil comes out the other end of the tube, it emerges point first, having apparently reversed itself inside the tube.

The pencil is sharpened on both ends. Then a piece of glazed paper is rolled around it, and glued to form a paper tube. The glazed covering should be just long enough so that one point of the pencil will extend.

In pushing the innocent looking pencil through the larger paper tube, the extending point is pushed into the glazed covering, so that the point will extend from the opposite end. Thus when the pencil comes out it will be reversed, coming out point first.

4. NAMING THE SUIT

A sheet of paper is laid on the table. The magician's assistant leaves the room. Some person is asked to name any suit of a pack of playing cards: diamonds, clubs, hearts, or spades.

When this has been done, the magician gives him a pencil and tells him to write "What suit did I choose?" or any other words that ask the same question. The person then takes the paper and pencil out to the assistant who immediately writes the name of the chosen suit.

Pencils are responsible for this trick. The magician has four different pencils in his pocket, each one representing a different suit. He merely gives the proper pencil to the spectator to take out to the assistant. When the assistant sees the pencil he knows the chosen suit.

5.   PENCIL FROM POCKETBOOK

A small purse is opened, and a pencil is drawn from its interior. The pencil is three times as long as the pocketbook.

The pencil is previously concealed up the sleeve, so that the tip of it comes into the palm of the hand. The back of the hand is towards the audience.

The bottom of the purse has an opening, so that when the purse is placed in the hand that hides the pencil, and the pocketbook is opened, the other hand can reach down through and draw out the pencil.

An ordinary purse may be used: in this case the pencil is drawn up in back of the purse; from a short distance it will appear to come from inside the purse.

6.   BREAKING THE PENCIL

This is really a paper and pencil trick; the paper used is a dollar bill, or a bill of larger denomination. The bill is folded in half, lengthways. A person is asked to hold the ends of a pencil, and the magician strikes the pencil with the creased edge of the bill. Suddenly he makes a mighty stroke, and the pencil snaps in half!

To do this, simply extend the forefinger while the hand is sweeping downward. The finger strikes the pencil and breaks it.

7.   PENCIL UNDER HANDKERCHIEF

The magician places a pencil under a handkerchief. Everyone can see the shape of the pencil. Suddenly the handkerchief is tossed aside and the pencil is gone!

Method: As soon as the pencil is under the cloth, extend the forefinger so that it holds up the handkerchief and appears to be the pencil. The hand is raised and the pencil drops down the sleeve. Then the handkerchief is tossed aside, and the pencil has vanished!

8. RISING RING ON PENCIL

Holding a pencil upright, the magician drops a borrowed finger-ring over it. Making mysterious passes with his other hand, he causes the ring to climb the pencil, descend, finally rise and fall free.

For this trick a pencil with a removable eraser is needed, the best type being the cap eraser that fits over the end of the pencil. A length of black thread is also required. One end of the thread is wound around a button of the magician's coat; the other end is attached to the pencil beneath the eraser, which holds the thread in place.

The thread is loose when the ring is dropped on the pencil, which is held with the eraser upward. By moving the pencil forward or backward, the thread can be drawn taut or relaxed, causing the ring to rise or fall, apparently under magical control.

9. THE RISING PENCIL

In this trick, a pencil mysteriously rises from the magician's fist, whenever he pushes the pencil into his closed hand. The pencil may later be given for examination.

The secret depends upon a black thread running from beneath the eraser of the pencil to a coat button exactly as with the "Rising Ring" just previously described. To make the pencil rise from the fist, it is thrust eraser end downward. Then a slight forward motion of the hand will cause the pencil to rise point first.

At the finish of the trick, the eraser is removed and handed with the pencil for examination. The thread drops loose and hangs unseen against the magician's coat.

10. THE FOUNTAIN PENCIL

A pencil is borrowed, and is squeezed in the right hand. A stream of water immediately issues from the top of the pencil.

In his hand, the magician holds a hollow rubber ball, which has a small hole in the side. The ball is first squeezed and then dipped in water to fill it. When the pencil is held upright, and the hole in the ball points upwards, pressure will produce the fountain.

The ball may be disposed of by drying the hands and the pencil with a handkerchief; or the rubber ball may be attached to a piece of cord elastic, which runs back under the coat so that the ball is released it will fly out of sight.

CHAPTER XIX

RING TRICKS

Tricks with rings cover a wide range, for there are rings of all sorts and sizes. The rings required for the following experiments are all easily obtained. Tricks with Chinese coins come under the head of ring tricks, and in such cases as they are required, plain metal washers may be used instead of the Oriental cash.

1. THE PHANTOM RING

A metal ring, some three inches in diameter, is employed in this trick. The ring is given for thorough examination. Then the magician allows his wrists to be tied with cord, leaving a length of string between the wrists. He takes the ring, turns his back for a few moments, and then shows his hands again. The ring is on the string between the wrists!

Two rings are used in the trick. They should be sufficiently large to pass over the hand and on to the wrist. Large bracelets may be used, but solid metal rings may be bought cheaply at a hardware store. One of these rings is on the performer's arm, under his sleeve. He exhibits the other ring, and as soon as his hands are tied, turns his back or steps out of sight. He quickly drops the examined ring into his pocket and lets the duplicate ring slide down his arm, over his hand, and onto the string. Then he steps out and shows that the miracle has been accomplished.

2. THE IMPROVED PHANTOM RING

The effect of this trick is the same as that of the last, but the ring is made of pliable rubber. A ring of this type is used with certain makes of vacuum cleaners, and costs very little. It will stand minute inspection, for it is unprepared.

This is the only ring used. When the magician turns away, he slides it over his hand, and pulls it *under* the loop of string that encircles his wrist. The string is then on his arm, and can be slipped over the hand and onto the wrist.

3. RING TIED ON STRING

The effect of this trick is the same as the effects of the last two; but a ring of any size may be used, and the ring is actually *tied* on the string between the wrists.

To accomplish this, gather up a loop of string between the wrists, thrust it through the center of the ring, and push the loop under the string that encircles the left hand. Then draw the loop over the left fingers and again push it under the string that encircles the left wrist. Once more pull the loop over the left fingers, and the ring will be tied on the string.

There should be plenty of string between the wrists. With a little practice the various movements can be effected in a very few seconds.

4. THE RING ON THE FINGER

In this trick, the magician's hands are tied behind his back, the wrists being firmly bound together. A finger ring is placed between the magician's teeth, and he steps behind a screen or out of the room. The spectators call out and designate one of the magician's fingers, or thumbs, and a moment later he appears, with the ring on the chosen finger, but with his wrists still firmly tied.

Method: As soon as he is out of sight, the magician swings his hands as far to the left as he can get them, so that the right hand is palm up. By turning his head to the left, he can let the ring drop from his teeth into the right hand. It is then an easy matter to slip the ring on any finger.

5. THE RING AND THE STRING

This is a simple trick, and one that can be performed very rapidly. Make a loop of string and thread a ring on it. Ask a spectator to extend his forefingers upward, and slip one end of the loop over each finger, so the forefingers hold the string with the ring between them. The problem is to remove the ring without taking the string from the person's fingers.

To do this, take hold of one string to the right of ring, and slip the string over the person's right finger, which will be to your left. Immediately remove the loop that was already over the right finger, and the ring will fall off, but the string will still run from finger to finger.

6. THE RELEASED RINGS

A ring is looped on a string, in the center. Then several other rings are dropped over both ends of the string, so that they slide down and are caught by the bottom ring. Some person holds both ends of the string, and a handkerchief is thrown over the rings. The magician immediately reaches under the cloth and removes the rings!

The secret lies in the manner in which the first ring is "tied" to the string. The two ends of the string are first pushed through the center of the ring. They are then run back through the loop at the center of the string, and the string is drawn tightly against the ring. To all appearances, the ring is tightly affixed to the string, but by taking hold of the loop and drawing it down the sides of the ring, the magician can release the ring. This is done underneath the cloth, and, of course, the other rings drop off when the supporting ring is removed.

7. THE VANISHING RING

The "vanishing" of a ring is not a difficult problem. Simply have a plain ring sewn in the corner of a large handkerchief. Borrow a ring and put it under the handkerchief. At the same time push up the corner of the handkerchief so that it may be gripped through the center of the cloth. Any person may take hold of the ring and satisfy himself that it is there, but he is holding the duplicate ring, while your hand calmly goes away with the original. When the handkerchief is shaken out, the ring will have vanished completely.

8. THE RING IN THE EGG

The Vanishing Ring trick, just explained, is most effective in combination with a trick wherein the borrowed ring is mysteriously reproduced. Such a trick is the Ring in the Egg.

After the borrowed ring has disappeared, an egg is broken, with a buttonhook, and the hook is inserted in the egg. A moment later the hook emerges, carrying the borrowed ring! The egg may be examined before the trick begins.

Method: While the audience is holding the handkerchief, which they believe holds the borrowed ring, you walk to a nearby table to get the buttonhook, and an egg cup. The egg cup has some wax or paraffine in the bottom. In picking up the cup, insert the ring edgewise in the bottom, so that it is imbedded in the wax. Bring forward the cup and the buttonhook. Take the egg and set it in the cup. The handkerchief is shaken, and the ring has vanished.

Holding the egg with the fingers of the left hand, break the top with the buttonhook, which is held by the right hand. At the same time, press down on the egg and the ring will be forced through the bottom. Thus the ring is actually in the egg, and may be produced on the end of the hook.

9. THE RING FROM THE STRING

This is one of the best of ring tricks. Preferably it should be performed with a Chinese coin or a washer, but a ring may be used.

The ring is threaded on a string, and the ends are held by two persons. Then a cloth is thrown over the ring. You reach under the cloth, and remove it a moment later, showing the ring is now tied to the string. Then, while the ends of the string are still held, you take the ring right off the string!

Two rings are used in the trick. The duplicate is concealed in the right hand. In reaching under the cloth, the hands gather a loop of the string and push it through the center of the loose ring. Then the loop is spread over the ring so that it is temporarily held to the string.

The left hand covers the original ring, which should be to the left of the duplicate. The right hand removes the cloth and everyone sees the duplicate ring, which they think is the original. At this point you carelessly slide your hands along the string to the ends, and momentarily take the ends away from the spectators so that you can hold the string up higher. You immediately put the ends back in their hands. This little procedure has, however, enabled you to draw the original ring right off the end of the string. While your left hand pockets the original ring, along with the handkerchief, the right hand mysteriously removes the ring from the center of the string.

10. THE CARDBOARD RING TRICK

The effect of this trick is identical with "The Ring From the String," but a ring, or washer, of cardboard is utilized instead of the metal article. A duplicate ring is used and is threaded on the string; but the original ring may be *torn off* and carried away when the handkerchief is removed, thus eliminating the subterfuge of sliding the hands along and off the ends of the string.

11. INSTANTANEOUS APPEARANCE OF SIX RINGS

Metal washers or Chinese coins should be used in this surprising trick. The magician holds out his right hand, with the palm towards the audience. The hand is obviously empty, but when he grasps in the air, he instantly catches half a dozen Chinese coins, which are tossed from hand to hand, and finally given for inspection.

The coins are first stacked together. A thread, white or pink, is then run through their centers, and tied in a loop. The loop should be long enough so that when it is slipped over the right thumb the coins will hang out of sight behind the hand.

With the coins in position, the palm of the hand may be shown quite empty, the thread being invisible at a distance of a few feet. Swing the hand upward, and tilt it slightly forward. The coins will fly over into the hand, where they are caught in the fist.

The coins may be tossed from hand to hand without breaking the thread, or they may be "vanished" from the right hand. This is done by letting the coins lie on the palm of the hand. Then the left hand covers the coins, and the left fingers push them over and in back of the right hand, where they hang out of sight, while both palms are shown. Then the coins may be caught again, and this time, the string is broken when the coins are passed from hand to hand, so the coins may be given for inspection.

12.   THE DROPPING RING

This experiment may be worked with a finger ring or a napkin ring. Take a circle of string and push one end through the center of the ring; then push the opposite end through the loop thus formed.

A reference to the diagram will show how the string appears. Let two persons take hold of the string at the point marked X

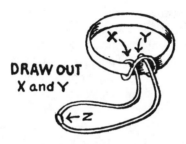

DRAW OUT
X and Y

and Y, while you hold the loop Z. When they pull the ends taut, the string will be held in three ways.

Have your other hand below the ring and say, "Pull." As the persons pull on the loops, let go of the loop you are holding, and the ring will drop into your outstretched hand.

CHAPTER XX

SPIRIT TRICKS

Under the classification of "Spirit Tricks" come those tricks which closely resemble so-called psychic phenomena.

These tricks should be presented only for entertainment, to demonstrate an interesting phase of modern magic.

Tricks of this type are very popular nowadays, and are well-suited to the impromptu performer, because they are supposed to be performed in the midst of a circle, or in a private home. Therefore they are very useful to the amateur magician.

The performance of such tricks and the fact that people can be mystified by them has no bearing upon the subject of psychic phenomena. That is a subject which must be carefully investigated by trained observers, and a detailed discussion of such matters is beyond the scope of this volume.

1. TWO MESSAGES

Two slates are shown, one at a time, and are placed together. A message appears on each slate.

A cardboard flap is used, painted black to match the slates. A message is on each slate, but one slate is lying with the message down and the other is covered with the flap.

The magician shows the covered slate, and lays it flap side up. He sets the second slate upon it and turns them both over. Then he removes the first slate and lays it with the message down. The flap now covers the message on the second slate, which may be shown on both sides. The second slate is laid on a table and the flap falls there. Then the two slates are quickly placed together, the messages coming between. Someone holds them and when they are taken apart, a message is seen on each slate.

2. POCKET SPIRIT SLATES

This is an excellent effect that can be shown anywhere—a great advantage for a trick of this type.

Two miniature slates are used. They are about two inches long by an inch across. They are shown blank on both sides; then they are placed together and encircled by a rubber band.

When the slates are opened, writing is seen on one of them. After the message has appeared the slates stand a close examination.

These slates can be made easily from cardboard, using several thicknesses of colored cardboard for the borders. But besides the slates, a "flap" is required, as in the case of the standard spirit slate trick. The flap is a loose piece of black cardboard which covers the message written on one of the slates, and makes the slate appear blank.

With these miniature slates, anyone can dispose of the cardboard flap without difficulty. The unprepared slate is shown on both sides. Then the prepared slate is shown and is laid on the left hand with the flap side down. The right hand picks it up and places it upon the unprepared slate. This action leaves the tiny flap behind in the left hand. The left hand immediately goes to the pocket and brings forth a rubber band to gird the slates. Thus the flap is secretly left in the pocket.

Another system is to wipe off the slates with a handkerchief, taking the tiny flap away with the handkerchief. The flap simply drops in the cloth where it is easily concealed.

The slates are not necessarily limited to the size mentioned;

they may be between three and four inches long and from two to three wide.

Very neat slates may be made from black fibre, with red fibre borders. Standard slates are not, of course, made in so small a size.

3. SINGLE SPIRIT SLATE

In this method, a message is obtained on a single slate, of fairly large size. It is shown blank on both sides and is placed in a paper bag. When it is removed, the message is on it; and the bag is crumpled and thrown away.

A flap is used; but it is made of a sheet of black tissue paper, which is not transparent. A message is written on one side of the slate, and it is covered with the tissue paper flap.

Both sides of the slate may then be shown; when the slate is put in the bag, the tissue paper falls off. When the slate is removed, there is the message, and the bag is easily rolled up and thrown away carrying the paper "flap".

Care must be taken to keep the paper covering on the slate while the slate is being shown. A few dabs of wax or soap will help this; but too much adhesive should not be used, otherwise the paper cannot be pushed off easily. The fingers can help to remove the paper when the slate goes in the bag.

Carbon paper makes an excellent substitute for black tissue.

4. THE SPIRIT BELL

The magician shows a small bell with a handle. He holds a cloth in front of the bell, and the bell mysteriously rings.

The bell has a hole in the handle, through which runs a piece of black thread. The ends of the thread are attached to corners of the handkerchief. When the handkerchief is held in front of the bell, and the upper edge of the cloth is drawn taut, the bell will be raised, and will begin to ring, when the magician shakes the cloth slightly.

The ends of the thread should be but loosely tied to the handkerchief so that when the magician withdraws the cloth he can detach the thread and let it run free of the bell.

Another method is to have a tiny hook or projection on the bell handle. The thread engages this when the handkerchief is placed in position, and the bell is easily released later on.

5. THE SPIRIT CLOTH

This is another method of making bells ring behind a cloth; but besides the bell, articles are upset or tossed in the air by an unseen force.

The trick must be worked quickly, as will be evident from the explanation.

On the upper right corner of the cloth, there is a bent pin. The magician stands to the left of the table upon which the articles are placed. He stretches out his right hand holding the cloth before the objects. Then he shows the other side of the cloth by extending his left hand and bringing his right hand in against his left shoulder. This allows him to quickly hook the corner of the cloth on the left shoulder of his coat. The cloth remains taut because of the extended left hand; and the right hand is free to manipulate the objects behind the cloth.

Then the right hand comes back to its corner, detaches the hook, and the cloth is shown held in both hands, as at the outset. The temporary release of the right hand cannot be observed from in front.

6. CHOOSING A QUESTION

In having messages appear upon slates, the magician must often decide upon something to write. For example, he can have the audience choose the name of a great man, and then the name appears upon a slate.

Or he can simply write something and seal it in an envelope; then he lets people select one of several cards with different names written thereon, and the chosen card will bear the name that the magician has written on the card in the envelope.

But how is the proper card chosen? That is done by means of a small bag, in which the magician drops cards bearing different names. The bag is easily made at home. It is like two bags sewn together—or better, an ordinary cloth bag with a cloth partition in the center. In one side are several cards all bearing the same name. When the magician holds the bag open, he spreads it so the secret side is not disclosed. The varying cards are dropped in, and the magician reopens the bag so that the secret pocket is now in view, and when anyone takes a card it must necessarily bear the desired name.

7. A SPIRIT ANSWER

The magician brings out a book, and asks a person to insert a card anywhere he chooses, in the book, thus determining a certain page.

A sealed envelope is handed to a spectator and then the book is opened at the indicated page. A person is told to read the first line.

The envelope is opened and inside is a card bearing the very words that the person has read!

Method: The book used must have a plain cover. The magician chooses a page and writes its first line on a card which he seals in an envelope. Then he inserts a card at that particular page of the book, but when he carries the book, his hand hides the projecting card.

A spectator thrusts a card in at the opposite end of the book. While he is handing the envelope to a person, the magician calmly turns over the book, revealing the other end, with *his own card* projecting. The spectator thinks that it is the card he inserted, and he opens the book at the right page. The magician, of course, secretly removes the spectator's card during the opening of the book.

8. SPIRIT TABLE LIFTING

This is a simple method whereby a table may apparently be lifted several feet in the air. A light table must be used.

People sit around the table and rest their hands lightly upon it. The magician presses forward on the table and inserts his foot beneath one leg. He presses with one hand directly over the leg, thus forming a clamp. When he raises his toe, the table will rise mysteriously. When the magician pushes it away from him, it will fall. The foot and the hand act as a sort of clamp that holds the table firmly.

9. ONE HAND TABLE LIFTING

The magician places his hand upon a light table, and when he lifts his hand, up comes the table. It may be raised to a height of several feet.

Then he places a handkerchief over the table; and puts his hand on it, but again the table comes up, although the presence of the silk handkerchief would seem to make any contact impossible.

Method: There is a small tack on the top of the table. The magician wears a ring, which has a small slot in it.*

The hand is placed on the table and the ring engages the tack. Lifting the table is then an easy matter. When the silk handkerchief is placed upon the table, it makes no difference. The ring engages the tack through the silk. At the finish, the magician pries out the tack with pressure of his hand, and lets the hand-

* The ring may be a plain one, painted a flesh-color. An ordinary finger-ring, however, does not appear suspicious.

kerchief fall over his hand. In removing the handkerchief he takes the ring also, so no trace remains.

10. AN EASY SLATE MESSAGE

The magician shows a blank slate and wraps it in a piece of newspaper. When the paper is opened, there is a message on the slate.

Method: The message is written in reverse on one side of the sheet of paper. That side is kept out of sight. When the paper is wrapped over the slate, the magician presses it against the slate, and thus transposes the message to the slate.

11. A SPIRIT QUESTION

A person is invited to write a question, fold it, and put it in a match-box, which the magician lays on the table.

He seats himself at the table, holds the match-box to his head, and slowly gives an answer to the written question.

Method: The magician obtains possession of the question by using a special match-box. A hole is cut in the bottom of the box and in the drawer, at one end.

The box is opened slightly at the other end, and the question is dropped in. When the box is closed the question falls through the bottom into the magician's hand.

He sits at the table, and with one hand beneath the table, opens the folded paper and reads it while he is holding the box to his forehead. Then he folds the paper again, and after he has answered the question, he finds an opportunity to push it back into the box.

12. STRANGE MANIFESTATIONS

The magician seats himself between two persons. He lets one person grip him by the right wrist, while with his left hand he holds the wrist of the person on his left. Then he has the lights turned out.

Immediately a horn is blown, a bell is rung, and raps are heard. The bell and horn are in front of the magician, but how can he operate them?

Then the lights are turned on, and everything is seen as before.

Method: Just as the lights are turned off, the magician draws his hands close together, and lets go of the person on the left for an instant, only to seize his wrist again. This time, however, he uses his right hand to take the person's wrist, leaving his left hand free to make the manifestations. Just before the lights are turned on he lets go with his right hand and grips the person's wrist with his left.

13. A SPIRIT GONG

The magician holds a metal gong in his hand, using a looped handkerchief as a handle by which to hold it; or he can use a glass bowl, with a handkerchief looped around the base.

In reply to questions, the gong rings mysteriously: once means "no"; twice means "yes".

The magician has a quantity of small shot in his hand. Each time he wishes to make the gong ring, he lets one ball of shot fall from his hand. The shot is not seen, but it makes the gong ring.

14. STRANGE TELEPATHY

The magician sits in a corner of the room, and blindfolds himself. Then he asks people to call out names of persons whose telephone numbers they know. As each name is called, the magician concentrates and slowly gives the telephone number.

An assistant is used. The magician sits in front of a door or a screen, and the assistant is behind him with a phone book, with index tabs so that he can quickly find numbers as the names are called. While the magician is "concentrating", the assistant looks up the number of a name that is called and whispers it to the magician who names it slowly and impressively.

15. MYSTERIOUS ANSWERS

The magician tells people that they can write questions and fold them up, while he is out of the room. Then he comes into the room and touches each person's forehead. This, he says, gives him their thoughts. He sits down, opens a book, and reads a few lines. Then he answers one of the questions. He repeats this, first reading and then answering questions until he has answered practically all of the written questions.

Method: The magician has a confederate—or two, if many people are present. The confederate pretends to write questions, but instead he watches what other people are writing, or listens to the other people talking over questions, and on his paper he writes the names of people and the questions they are asking. When the magician enters and walks among the people, the confederate secretly drops the information in the magician's pocket; or he can place it in the pages of the book the magician intends to use. When the magician opens the book he gains the necessary information. Of course he can also answer an imaginary question which the confederate will claim to be the one he wrote.

16. MIND READING

In this trick the magician employs a "medium" who is seated across the room, and is blindfolded.

The magician states that he can send thoughts of various objects to the medium by picturing them. He asks persons to have the objects ready, such as coins, rings, pins, etc.

Then he walks around touching the various objects, and as he touches each one, the medium names it.

SPIRIT TRICKS

This is done by having a rotation of objects, such as ring, coin, pin, watch, shoe, glasses, book, match-box, etc. The magician touches these in the memorized order, so that as he says "Name this", the medium knows what to say. Various objects, such as books and match-boxes can be laying around where the magician can hold them up if they are not offered to him.

If he wishes, the magician can say: "That's right", after the medium names an object such as a watch. That means "repeat", and the magician immediately holds up another watch. If he simply says "Right", the medium knows that he is going to eliminate the next object in the prearranged order. Thus if he touches a person's shoe, and the medium names it, the magician, if he sees no eyeglasses, will say "Right". So the next object he touches will be a book.

The two persons who work the trick can best arrange their own system of rotation.

17. THE MYSTIC RING

A metal ring is laid upon the table. It is about the size of a large bracelet.

The magician turns out the light with one hand and immediately grasps the person's hand with his other hand. Then he states that in a few seconds the ring will mysteriously leap on to the person's arm, although that would seem impossible, as the magician is holding the person's hand.

Suddenly the person feels the ring. The magician turns on the light and there is the ring, on the person's arm!

Method: As soon as he turns off the light the magician seizes the ring with his free hand and lets it slide on to his wrist.

Then he seizes the person's hand, and a little while later he tilts his hand so that the ring slides off his wrist on to the person's arm, passing over both hands.

18. A CLEVER SLATE WRITING TRICK

This method of slate writing requires nerve; but when properly performed it is very mystifying.

The magician writes a few words on a slate and then rubs them off. He asks for a question, and in order to visualize it, he writes it slowly word for word on the slate.

Then he rubs it off again, and lays the slate on the table, with the chalk upon it.

A few minutes later he turns over the slate and there is the answer to the question written on it!

Method: When the magician slowly writes the question, he really writes a suitable answer, and only pretends to rub away the writing. He lays the slate with the writing side down, and of course when it is turned over the answer is found on it!

19. THE TAPED SLATES

Two slates are bound with a piece of tape which runs crosswise about them. The surface of one slate is marked with a figure 1; then the slates are turned over and the other is marked with a figure 2. The slates are untied, and the inner surfaces are shown, one being marked 3 and the other 4. Then the slates are tied together with the tape. When they are untied, a message is found between them, written on one of the slates.

The message, or written word, is on the slate at the beginning. It is on the side of the upper slate marked 1. It is written lengthwise along the slate with a sharp chalk or slate pencil, and the letters are just small enough to be concealed by the ribbon which is around the slates.

When the tied slates are shown and the outer surfaces are marked 1 and 2, no one supposes that the ribbon hides anything. When the slates are unbound, the side marked 1 is laid down on the table, the side 2 being up. Thus side 2 is seen; that slate is turned over and the inner sides are marked 3 and 4. Then one slate is laid with side 2 up; and the other slate is placed upon it, so that side 1 comes over side 2, while 3 and 4 become the outsides of the slates.

The slates are tied up in the tape, which is later removed and the message is found. The letters of the message appear much higher than the width of the ribbon.

The trick may be performed with two slabs of cardboard, the message appearing in ink.

20. THE THREE SPIRIT SLATES

This is a stock item among magicians, but it is usually performed with two slates. The addition of the third slate is a great improvement.

The magician shows both sides of three slates. Then he asks that one slate be chosen. This slate he discards, tucking it under his left arm. He numbers the other slates 1 and 2, and places them together with the numbers on the outside. When the slates are taken apart, a message appears on the inner surface of one slate. The slate is given for examination, and the other slate is also handed for inspection.

Beside the slates, a black flap is used, made of silicate or of cardboard. It lies on one of the slates, and covers the message, which is written previously. The flap is just the size of the slate minus the frame, so it hides the message perfectly.

When the magician shows the three slates on both sides, he asks that one be selected. If it is not the flap slate, he puts the chosen slate under his left arm saying that that slate will be eliminated. If, however, the flap slate is chosen, he says: "I will use this slate, and one of the others. Which of the other two slates do you choose?"

Thus one of the two odd slates finds its way under the left arm.

The flap slate and the unprepared slate are placed together and they are turned over, which lets the flap fall on the unprepared slate. The slates are laid on the table, and the upper slate is turned over, showing the message. The flap lies on the blank slate.

Without hesitation, the magician pushes forward the slate with the message. Then he picks up the blank slate with his left hand, and with his right hand, takes the third slate from under his left arm. He sets the third slate on the slate that has the flap, and turns the two slates over, thus transferring the flap to the odd third slate, which is immediately replaced under the left arm. Then the second slate, rid of the flap, is laid on the table for inspection.

"Getting rid of the flap" is considered the most difficult part of the slate trick. This method makes it very easy, and enables the magician to walk away with the flap on the innocent third slate leaving the two numbered slates in the possession of the audience.

21. THE SPIRIT NAME

This is a trick that requires careful observation. After it has been tried a few times, it seldom fails to work.

Tell a person to think of a spirit name—of some celebrity, if he wishes.

Then tell him that he is to write down a list of names on a sheet of paper, and somewhere in the list he must place the name upon which he is concentrating. Eight or ten names will be enough. Before beginning, he should determine mentally at what number he will write the chosen name.

The person writes down the names, while you are looking on. When he has finished, you hold his hand and look at the list. Then you immediately pick out the spirit name of which he was thinking.

Method: While the person is writing down the names, he will

generally hesitate to think of what name he will write next. But when he comes to the point where he has intended to write the chosen name, he will write it without hesitation. Thus you can tell which name is the chosen one.

22. THE SPIRIT HAND

The magician holds both his forefingers in front of a person's eyes, and tells the person to close his eyelids. Then the tips of the forefingers are set against the eyelids.

"Can you feel both of my forefingers?" asks the magician.

"Yes," is the reply.

"Then," says the magician, "since both of my hands are occupied, I will call upon a spirit hand to aid me."

At this instant an unknown hand brushes the person's hair, and taps his forehead. The magician immediately removes his hands and the spectator may open his eyes. But no one else is nearby. There seems to be no explanation of the spirit touch.

This trick is done very artfully. As soon as the person shuts his eyes, the magician extends the first two fingers of one hand, spreads them and places one against each of the person's eyelids. This leaves the magician's other hand free to act as the spirit hand. When the fingers are removed from the eyelids, both hands are held with forefingers extended.

23. CONTACT TELEPATHY

This is an interesting experiment performed by two people. One acts as the transmitter of thoughts. He is told a number, while the receiving person is out of the room. Then the transmitter is seated in a corner, with his back towards the room. The receiver is brought in, blindfolded. He is allowed to place the tips of his forefingers upon the temples of the transmitter. A few moments later the receiver announces the number!

There is no mind reading to it. The transmitter signals to the receiver by a very artful system. By simply tightening his lower jaw, the transmitter causes his temples to press slightly against the receiver's forefingers. In this manner the receiver is informed of the number. Suppose the number was 153. The transmitter would press his jaw once, signifying one; then after a slight interval, he would make five presses; then another interval, and three presses. Thus any number of moderate length can be "transmitted" quickly and undetectably.

Ten presses signify zero.

24. READING SEALED MESSAGE

A name is written on a slip of paper, which is put, written side down, into an envelope. The envelope is sealed.

Holding the envelope to his forehead the magician instantly names the written name.

Method: A flap is cut in the face of the envelope. This side of the envelope is down, so the cut is not seen. When the message is inside, the magician raises the envelope to his forehead. At the same time his thumb lifts up the flap and he sees the written name.

25. IMPROVED ENVELOPE TEST

This is the most effective of all sealed envelope readings. Take a few envelopes and glue them together. Cut out a space in the center of the envelopes large enough to hold a small tobacco tin. The tin contains a sponge, saturated with alcohol.

A number of genuine envelopes are places upon the dummy stack, and, of course the bottom envelope of the dummy pile is complete. Thus the hidden sponge cannot be seen.

A number of envelopes are given out, with slips of paper. Names are written on these slips which must be inserted, writing down, in the envelopes. The magician gathers up the envelopes, and adds them to those he still has, so that the envelopes containing the questions come directly on top of the alcohol sponge.

The magician then draws out the lowermost of the question envelopes and holds it to his forehead. The alcohol renders it transparent and the magician can read the name or message that is within. This is repeated with all the remaining questions. The envelopes should be laid on the table, leaning against a lamp, which will quickly dry the alcohol, and make the envelopes opaque once more.

26. THE GREAT ROPE TIE

The magician is seated in a chair behind a screen. His arms are crossed, ropes are tied about his wrists, and the ends of the cords are fastened to the chair rungs.

As soon as everyone has left him alone, bells, placed beside the magician, begin to ring. Articles are tossed over the screen. But a half-minute later, when the magician invites people back to see him, he is tied as securely as before. He must be untied to be released.

The magician does not escape from the ties at all, but he does release himself sufficiently to ring the bells and throw things from behind the screen. By sliding down in the chair, the magician can raise one arm over his head, and can then slip under the other arm. Thus he is partially free. After ringing the bells, he slides back into the ropes just as he was before. As the ropes have not been tampered with, the inference is that some unseen force, and not the magician, rang the bells.

The magician can also tie a ring on the string, as an additional effect. (See "Ring Tied on String," Chapter XIX.)

CHAPTER XXI

STRING TRICKS

1. THE REMOVABLE STRING

Take off your coat, and hang a long loop of string over your arm. Then put your right hand in your right vest pocket. The problem is to remove the string without taking the hand from the pocket.

To do it, take hold of the loop with your left hand and pull it up through the right armhole of your vest. Slide the loop over your head, push it through the left armhole and put your left arm through it. The string will then be around your body, beneath your vest. Reach up under the vest with the left arm; get hold of the string and pull it down your body. Then step out of it.

If some one else attempts the trick, he will probably get all tangled up, especially if he makes the common mistake of putting his right hand in his trousers pocket instead of in the vest pocket.

2. A RESTORED STRING

A string is pushed through a drinking straw, and the straw is bent in the center. The magician cuts the center of the straw, and then draws the pieces away, showing the string as good as ever!

Method: Have a tiny section of a straw bent and concealed between the fingers of the right hand.

Insert the string in the genuine straw and bend the straw. Bring up your right hand and add the section, holding the join between your left thumb and fingers. The spectators will see what appears to be the center of the straw. With scissors, cut off the fake section, and bring the hands together, to break the real straw. Draw the two sections apart, and reveal the string uncut.

3. SCISSORS AND STRING

A string is run through one of the handles of a pair of scissors. The string is tied in a loop and the knot is held by a spectator. The magician states that he will remove the scissors from the string without untying the knot or without doing anything but manipulate the scissors.

There is a catch to this one. The loop is long. The magician can manipulate the scissors, and he does it by turning up the scissors and cutting the string!

4. STRING AND ICE CUBE

Float an ice cube in a glass of water, take a string and tie a loop in one end. Then invite people to snare the ice cube with the string and lift the cube from the glass.

The more they try, the more they will fail, because looping the ice cube is just about impossible. But when your turn comes, you can lift the ice with the string—by working it your own special way.

Simply let the wet loop rest on the ice cube. Sprinkle a little salt on the ice. The surface will melt rapidly, then freeze again with the string imbedded in it. Lift the string carefully by the free end and you can draw the ice cube out of the glass.

5. CUT THE CENTER

A long string is tied to the handle of a china cup so that the cup can be dangled by the string. The magician states that he can cut the string in the center, actually dividing it into two pieces, yet the string will still support the cup. This can be done while the cup is dangling from the string.

This sounds impossible, so the magician does it. He lets someone else hold the string with the hanging cup. Then he takes the center of the string and ties a loop in it, pulling the knot quite tight.

Next, the magician cuts the center of the loop and the trick is thereby accomplished. The string has actually been cut in two, but it still supports the cup, thanks to the helpful knot!

6. ON AND OFF LOOP

The magician hangs a loop of string over his right thumb and forefinger, places the tips of thumb and forefinger together, and suddenly draws the string completely clear with his left hand, though it appears to be intricately looped on the right.

The necessary maneuvers are very simple, but extremely deceptive. Extend the left thumb and forefinger horizontally, keeping them spread to form a V. With the left hand hang the loop on the right thumb and forefinger.

Now with the left hand, reach up into the V and pull the cross-string clear down, thus forming separate loops on the right thumb and forefinger. With the left hand, draw the dangling loop (the original cross-string) up through the V. Then press the tips of the right thumb and forefinger together, forming a circle, which seems to snare the loops completely.

But the left hand, never releasing the long loop, has only to draw it over the right thumb and forefinger. The entire string will be carried free of the right hand.

CHAPTER XXII

SUGAR TRICKS

1. FLOATING SUGAR

This is an interesting experiment with a lump of sugar. The lump is dropped in a cup of liquid, and of course it sinks to the bottom. But, a few moments later, the sugar suddenly rises to the surface of the liquid and floats there!

The lump of sugar is an ordinary cube of sugar, which has first been dipped in liquid collodion. When the lump is dry, it appears unchanged. When it is dropped into liquid, the sugar melts; but the collodion preserves the shape of the lump and up it comes to the top.

2. BURNING SUGAR

Ask a person to set fire to a lump of sugar. He will be unable to do so. The flame of the match will merely blacken the sugar. But when you apply a match to a lump, the sugar burns with a tiny blue flame.

Sugar contains alcohol, and it will burn provided the combustion is once started. To do this, secretly dip the corner of the lump into cigarette or cigar ashes; then apply the match, and the sugar will burn.

3. THE CLOUD OF SUGAR

This trick has been attributed to the Hindu fakirs. A mouthful of sugar is taken from a spoon, and suddenly it is blown

209

forth in a dry cloud. This is particularly effective when colored sugars are used, as two or three clouds may be blown.

The dry sugar is contained in a large capsule, which has pin-holes at the ends. It is taken into the mouth with the spoonful of sugar. The loose sugar dissolves, of course; but the capsule is held between the lips, and by blowing through it, the cloud of sugar is formed.

4. THE MYSTIC LETTER

This is a very interesting problem in mystery. A person is requested to write an initial or a figure on a lump of sugar, and to lay the lump with the letter down. The magician takes the lump of sugar, and without looking at it, drops it in a glass of water. He tells the person to close his fist, then holds the glass of water above the spectator's clenched hand. After the sugar is partly dissolved, the magician tells the spectator to open his fist and there on the palm of the hand, is the imprint of the letter on the sugar, perfectly reproduced!

Now for the secret, which is quite artful. While the spectator is writing the initial, the magician secretly moistens the ball of his right thumb; this can often be done by merely rubbing the thumb along the outside of the glass. Just a bit of dampness is required.

In picking up the lump of sugar, the magician presses his thumb against the initial side; then he drops the sugar in the glass. The imprint of the letter remains on the magician's thumb. With both of his hands, the magician grasps the spectator's hand and closes it into a fist. In so doing, the magician's thumb presses against the person's palm, and thus leaves the imprint of the initial.

SUGAR TRICKS

5. TRAVELING LUMPS OF SUGAR

This is one of the finest of all impromptu tricks—it is admirably suited to the dinner table, and it can be learned without a great deal of practice.

The magician lays four lumps of sugar on the table, so that they form the corners of a square.

He covers two lumps of sugar, one with each hand, and wiggles his fingers. When he lifts his hands, *two lumps* are beneath the left, while the *lump of sugar has gone* from the right!

Without hesitating, the magician places one hand over a single lump, and the other hand over the two lumps. Again the single lump passes, and three lumps appear together!

The last single lump is covered, and all four lumps appear together!

The process is immediately reversed. The four lumps are covered with one hand, and the other hand is placed at one of the empty corners of the imaginary square. When the hands are lifted, one lump is back at the corner, and only three remain in the group. This is repeated, until there is a lump at every corner. Then the hands are shown empty and the sugar may be examined.

Method: We will call the lumps of sugar A, B, C, and D. Besides them, there is an extra lump of sugar which is hidden in the left palm. It is held there by pressure at the base of the thumb, and with a little practice it can be retained with ease.

The right hand arranges the visible lumps thus:

D   C

B   A

Everything is ready for action. Each movement must follow quickly after the one before.

The right hand is placed over lump A; the left over D. The fingers are wiggled, and the right hand "palms" A, while the left hand leaves its lump with D. The hands are raised (without showing the palms) and lump A has disappeared, two lumps being at D.

The left hand immediately covers B, while the right goes to D. The fingers are wiggled, and are lifted, the left palm gripping lump B, while the right hand leaves the lump that it carried from A.

The empty right hand now covers C, while the left hand covers the three lumps at D. When the hands are lifted, the right hand picks up C, and the left hand leaves the fourth lump at D.

The process is immediately reversed. The left hand covers the four lumps and picks up one, while the right hand deposits a lump at C. The left hand goes to B, and leaves its lump there while the right hand is covering the three lumps and removing one from D. Then the right hand goes to A and leaves the lump there while the left picks up one of the two lumps at D.

The left hand is lifted an instant before the right; and as the eyes of the spectators naturally go to the right hand, the left hand drops the odd lump of sugar in the lap or in the pocket.

6. SUGAR THROUGH TABLE

Taking a wrapped lump of sugar, the magician stands it on the dinner table and sets a glass of water on top of the sugar lump. Placing his right hand over the mouth of the glass, he puts his left hand beneath the table and suddenly drives the glass down upon the table with his right hand. The left hand immediately emerges from beneath and tosses the lump of sugar on the table.

Apparently the solid sugar lump has been driven right through the table. As proof of same, the magician lifts the glass and beneath it is found the crumpled sugar wrapper, which can be opened and shown entirely devoid of sugar.

This novel trick depends upon an unsuspected fact; namely, that an empty sugar wrapper is strong enough to support the weight of a glass of water. Beforehand, the magician removes a lump from its wrapper and places the latter—all closed again—in the sugar bowl. This is the "lump" that he uses in the trick.

The tips of the right fingers can steady the glass lightly when it is set upon the empty wrapper, care being taken to convince the spectators that the full weight is actually supported by the supposedly wrapped lump. In his lap, the performer has the actual lump of sugar and it is brought up by the left hand after the glass has "driven" it through the table.

CHAPTER XXIII

TABLE TRICKS

1. THE MAGNETIC KNIFE

A table knife is placed against the palm of the hand. It remains there, as though magnetized to the hand, which is held in a vertical position, with the fingers pointing straight forward.

To do this, you need the proper kind of a knife and you must study the correct position. Set the knife point downward against the fingers of the left hand. The knife must have a heavy handle, with a bulge where the blade starts; and this bulge, or projection, rests upon the joint of the left little finger. The hand is not quite vertical; it is tilted backward imperceptibly. The weight of the handle rests against the fingers, and the knife sets firmly in position, although its situation seems precarious.

2. THE OBEDIENT SPOON

A spoon is placed upon the tips of the fingers, and it remains there for a short time. At the performer's command, the spoon suddenly turns over!

The spoon has a hump in the handle; and it is set on the fingers so that the hump is downward. The spoon is actually balanced there, but it is not difficult to keep it from turning over.

When the hand is tilted imperceptibly, the spoon loses its balance, and turns over—apparently of its own accord!

3. THE JUMPING CANDLE FLAME

This trick can be performed anywhere; but when there are candles on the table, it makes a good dinner-table trick.

The magician lights a match from the candle flame. Then he blows out the candle. A moment later he holds the match above the candle-wick, and to the surprise of everyone, a portion of the flame leaves the match and jumps to the candle, where it immediately lights the wick!

The secret lies in watching the curl of thin smoke that goes up from the candle immediately after it has been blown out. Set the match flame so that it encounters this slender stream of smoke, and the flame will travel down to the wick in a most astonishing fashion. Sometimes a candle may be reignited this way several minutes after it has been extinguished; and the flame will often travel a distance of several inches.

4. VANISHING SALT

A napkin ring is laid upon the table, and salt is poured into it. A small piece of cardboard is laid over the ring, and the ring is lifted. The salt is gone!

Method: Take a circular piece of white paper and glue it to the bottom of the napkin ring. This paper matches the table-cloth and will not be detected. When salt is poured in and the ring lifted, the salt comes along. The piece of cardboard hides the salt in the ring. The ring should be pocketed, with the salt.

5. THE ENCHANTED SEED

A grape seed is dropped into a glass of ginger-ale. It sinks to the bottom of the liquid.

At the magician's command, the seed rises to the top of the

glass, and remains there until he tells it to sink. Down it goes again, and comes up when it is told to rise.

This is a very curious and interesting experiment. It is caused by the air-bubbles in the ginger-ale. The seed naturally sinks, but as soon as a few bubbles cluster around it, it comes to the top. There the air-bubbles escape, and down goes the seed, only to rise again in a few moments.

The performer must time his commands when he has observed the bubbles forming or disappearing; yet the average onlooker will not detect the cause of the peculiar behavior of the seed.

6. THE ORANGE TO THE APPLE

Changing an orange to an apple is not a difficult trick—if you know the secret. The orange is placed beneath a napkin, and when the cloth is removed, there is the apple instead!

Method: Cut an orange into quarters and carefully remove the peel. Fix them around an apple, and if you do a neat job, no one will suspect that the fruit is not a genuine orange.

When the supposed orange has been covered with the napkin, reach beneath and quickly remove the peels, carrying them away in the folds of the napkin, leaving the apple there instead.

7. THE VANISHING KNIFE

A table knife is wrapped in a napkin. The napkin is rolled up and then unrolled. The knife is gone!

Method: Roll the napkin around the knife, and have the handle of the knife toward the edge of the table. The napkin is rolled loosely, and in tilting it up, the knife slides out, unobserved into the lap.

Another napkin should be on the lap to keep the knife from falling to the floor.

TABLE TRICKS

8. SWALLOWING A KNIFE

A knife is placed on the table, parallel to the edge. The magician picks up the knife with both hands, and appears to swallow it. The knife is gone!

This is done in picking up the knife. The hands are placed upon it, finger tips to finger tips. This position is taken two or three times, and finally the hands appear to scoop up the knife; but as they do so, they slide it to the edge of the table and let it fall into the lap. The hands are immediately raised to the mouth.

If this is done neatly, all eyes will follow the hands, thinking the knife is still there.

9. FIVE KNIFE TRICK

Five knives are laid upon the table. The object is to raise four of them with the other knife.

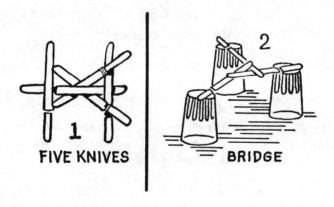

FIVE KNIVES | BRIDGE

This sounds impossible; but the magician can do it. It is very easily accomplished by following the illustration. (See Fig. 1.)

10. THE BRIDGE OF KNIVES

Using three tumblers as bases, the magician states that he can form a three-way bridge, with three knives, each one coming from its base—an inverted glass.

This is accomplished in the manner shown in Fig. 2. The blades of the knives are interlocked, and the handles rest upon the tumblers.

Note: There are various other tricks which appear in different chapters that are suited for use as "Table Tricks." They have been placed in their proper groups, and will be easily recognized by the reader.

11. BLOWING THROUGH A BOTTLE

A candle is lighted and is set on one side of a bottle. The magician blows against the bottle, and the candle is extinguished. He has, apparently, blown through the solid bottle!

A round bottle must be used. When the magician blows against it, the air currents are divided; but they rejoin on the other side to extinguish the candle. Two or three bottles or a bottle and a glass may be used. The result will always be the same.

12. THE RIBBON FROM THE ORANGE

This is a very effective dinner-table trick which should be performed with a small orange. You cut open the end of the orange, and produce a long coil of colored ribbon.

The ribbon actually comes from the orange; but it is not there at the beginning of the trick. It is threaded to a large needle, and is then coiled about the needle. The coil of ribbon is held in the left hand, with the point of the needle extending in from the palm, and the left hand is held beneath the table.

The right hand picks up the orange and in transferring it to the left hand, presses it down on the needle, which goes up through the center of the orange. In cutting into the orange, get hold of the needle and draw it out, bringing the ribbon along. The needle is easily concealed in the right hand as it pulls out the ribbon. Keep on pulling until the whole coil comes out; then, in smoothing the ribbon, slide the needle off and let it fall to the floor.

13. BOTTLE AND STRAW

Here the magician offers to lift a bottle with a straw!

It is a remarkable task, indeed; but it is easy of accomplishment. The straw is bent so as to make a short section, and it is pushed into the bottle, at the bend. The short section springs out and acts as a lever or catch by which the bottle is lifted when the straw is raised.

14. KNIFE FROM THE GLASS

A pen-knife is shown and opened. It is placed in the center of a handkerchief and set in a glass, after the blade has been closed.

The handkerchief is whisked away, and the glass is empty.

When the knife is closed, it is lying on the handkerchief, and the magician takes care to catch some of the cloth in the blade.

In this manner the knife is attached to the handkerchief, so when it is quickly whisked away and pocketed, the knife comes with it.

Practically all the tricks in the chapters on "Sugar Tricks" and "Tumbler Tricks" are intended for the dinner table, but as there are many of them, they are treated in a separate chapter.

CHAPTER XXIV

THIMBLE TRICKS

1. A VANISHING THIMBLE

A thimble is placed on the finger tip of the right hand and is removed by the left hand. When the left hand is opened, the thimble has disappeared. The thimble is originally on the second finger of the right hand, while the other fingers are bent in. When the right hand is swung over to the left, the second finger is bent in, and the forefinger is extended in its place. The left hand immediately closes around the forefinger and pretends to draw away the thimble. The forefinger is seen without the thimble; so everyone supposes that the thimble is in the left hand. But when the hand is opened the thimble is gone.

The thimble may be drawn from the left elbow, on the tip of the second finger.

2. COLOR–CHANGING THIMBLE

This is a variation of the preceding trick. A red thimble is placed on the tip of the right forefinger and a blue one on the tip of the second finger. The blue thimble is shown and is apparently placed in the left hand. But again the fingers change positions, during the motion of the right hand, and when the left hand is opened, a red thimble is there instead of a blue.

3. THE JUMPING THIMBLE

A thimble is shown on the tip of the second finger of the right hand. The left hand is also shown, but it has no thimble. The hands are waved, and the thimble jumps from the right hand to the left, and back again.

Take a thin metal thimble and saw it or cut it in half, from top to bottom. Put one portion on the front of the right second finger, and the other portion on the back of the left second finger. By pressing the bottom edges of the half-thimbles, the magician can clamp them firmly to the finger tips.

Now, when the palms of the hands are shown, there will be a thimble on the tip of the right second finger; but none will be in view on the left.

In waving the hands, turn the backs towards the spectators, and the left-hand thimble will come into view while the right-hand thimble will be out of sight. Another wave of the hands brings the palms front and the thimble is back on the right.

4. THIMBLE FROM PAPER

A small sheet of paper is shown on both sides. It is rolled into a cone. The right forefinger is inserted in the cone, and comes out bearing a thimble.

The thimble is originally on the right forefinger. The paper is held at one end by the right forefinger, beneath, and the right thumb, above. The left hand grips the other end of the paper, and folds it over so that it covers the right thumb, which then releases the under end so that it springs forward. The right forefinger immediately comes up beneath the end held by the left hand, and the right thumb is set on top. Thus both sides of the paper are exhibited without revealing the thimble.

The left hand rolls the paper in a cone around the right forefinger, which is withdrawn, leaving the thimble in the cone. The finger is shown, and is carefully inserted in the cone, emerging with the thimble.

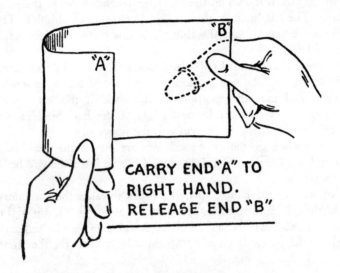

CARRY END "A" TO
RIGHT HAND.
RELEASE END "B"

5. THIMBLE THROUGH HANDKERCHIEF

The magician borrows a handkerchief and places a thimble beneath it, holding the thimble on the tip of his forefinger. He squeezes the handkerchief, and the thimble goes half way through it, so that both sides of the cloth may be shown, with the thimble extending through.

Then the thimble is pushed back, and the handkerchief is returned, uninjured.

Two thimbles are required for the trick. One must fit loosely over the other. The tip of the larger thimble is cut off, just at the bottom of the rough part. When this thimble is placed on the smaller thimble, the thimble appears quite ordinary, at a short distance.

In working, show the thimble, and place it temporarily in the left fist. Then take the thimble on the right forefinger, leaving the false tip in the left hand. Place the right hand under the cloth, with the forefinger extended, and insert the forefinger into the left fist, picking up the false tip. The handkerchief can then be shown with the thimble apparently half way through it!

Then place the left fist over the right forefinger and remove the false tip. Withdraw the handkerchief and show the thimble. Push the thimble into the left fist, and leave the false tip on it, so the hands may be shown empty, except for the thimble. It is an easy matter to dispose of the false tip after this.

6. COMPLETE PENETRATION

This is a good trick to work in connection with the previous item, as only the thimble itself is used, and it apparently passes right through the handkerchief.

The thimble is set on the tip of the forefinger, which is held upright, and a handkerchief is set over it. The back of the right hand is towards the audience and the left hand approaches in front of the extended finger, with the back of the left hand also towards the audience.

Now, the finger which is extended under the cloth is in reality the second finger, which has been raised instead of the forefinger. So as soon as the left hand covers in front of the handkerchief, the forefinger is raised up under the hem, and comes up in back of the handkerchief. As the left fist is closed, it encircles both the forefinger and the second finger, and grips the thimble. The left hand is raised slightly, to set the thimble on the second finger, through the cloth. The forefinger is immediately bent down. Then the left hand is removed, and there is the thimble through the handkerchief.

The left hand takes off the thimble. Then the handkerchief is given for examination, and the right hand is shown empty.

7. THE FLOATING THIMBLE

The magician demonstrates that a thimble will float—like a little boat—when he places it in a dish of water. A little push, however, and the thimble fills with water and sinks.

It is dried and someone else is asked to make it float. By this time the thimble sinks immediately! When the magician takes it again, it floats!

Method: *Two* thimbles are used, one a heavy nickel-plated or silver thimble; the other a light one, preferably of aluminum. These thimbles must look very much alike. The light one will float, the heavy one will not.

One thimble is concealed in the folds of the handkerchief that is used to dry the thimble. The act of drying enables the magician to secretly exchange one thimble for the other in an indetectible manner; thus he can make the thimble sink or float as he chooses.

Two light thimbles can be used, a few drops of solder being placed within one, to make it too heavy to float.

8. HANDKERCHIEF THROUGH THIMBLE

The magician shows one thimble on his right forefinger. Otherwise his hands are empty. He places a silk handkerchief over his forefinger, and reaching beneath the cloth with his left hand, brings out the thimble and sets it on his right forefinger, but with the cloth between the thimble and the finger.

Taking the handkerchief by all four corners, the magician yanks it with his left hand, and the handkerchief comes away, leaving the thimble still on the right forefinger! The effect of this is most startling.

It is accomplished by the use of two thimbles; one fits easily inside the other and they are shown as one on the tip of the right forefinger.

THIMBLE TRICKS

The cloth is spread over the right forefinger and the left hand brings the larger thimble out from beneath and sets it on top of the silk handkerchief. Thus the larger thimble covers the smaller, but with the cloth between. When the handkerchief is snatched away, the large thimble comes with it, but the smaller thimble is revealed on the right forefinger. The action is instantaneous and surprising.

The handkerchief is dropped in the coat pocket where the thimble falls from it.

9. MAGNETIC THIMBLES

Two thimbles are placed mouth to mouth. The upper thimble is held and the lower one adheres to it in a mysterious fashion. The thimbles are later shown to be quite ordinary.

Method: A little ball of spongy rubber is required. It is slightly greater in diameter than the opening of the thimble.

The ball is placed in one thimble, to a very slight degree, but it is kept hidden by the fingers. When the thimbles are placed mouth to mouth, the second thimble is forced over the ball, and the ball holds both firmly together.

When the thimbles are taken apart, they are immediately placed on the forefingers for exhibition. The ball of spongy rubber compresses and is forced up into the tip of one thimble, so the thimbles appear quite ordinary. Large thimbles should be used.

10. THE TELL–TALE THIMBLES

A tiny ball of paper is laid on the table, and is covered with one of three thimbles. The magician requests the spectators to cover the ball with any one thimble, while his back is turned, and then to mix the thimbles around on the table.

This is done; and the magician immediately points out the thimble which covers the paper ball!

There is no preparation about the thimbles. But in making the little ball, a short hair is rolled up in it, so that one end of the hair projects a short distance.

When the paper ball is on the table, no one will notice the presence of the hair. But when the thimbles are set on the table, the magician can instantly name the location of the paper ball by pointing out the thimble which has a bit of hair extending from beneath it.

11. RED, WHITE AND BLUE

This trick is similar to the last; except that three tissue-paper balls are used: red, white, and blue.

The magician can point out the location of each ball, when the balls have been covered by thimbles.

The red ball has a long hair, the paper being wrapped around the center. Thus two hairs will project from each side of the thimble covering the red ball. One hair projects from the thimble covering the white ball; while the blue ball is unprepared and nothing reveals its presence.

The balls can be carefully made, and glued so that the hairs will not come loose.

CHAPTER XXV

TUMBLER TRICKS

There are many interesting tricks in which drinking glasses are used, and some of them have been chosen for this chapter. They make excellent tricks for the dinner table, but they can be performed in other places as well.

1. THE OVER–FULL TUMBLER

How can a glass be more than full?

Very easily, as you will learn when you try this trick.

Take a glass and fill it to the brim, until everyone admits that it is quite full.

Then take another glass or a pitcher and very carefully pour a little bit of water into the full glass. If you do this slowly, the full glass will receive a small quantity of water.

Then if you look at the full glass from the side, you will observe that it is actually more than full. The water will be piled up in the center of the glass and will form a tiny hump which is quite visible. That is, the water will be above the brim of the glass!

Care must be taken that the brim of the glass does not become at all wet.

2. A TWO TUMBLER TRICK

The performer states that he will pour a quantity of water into a glass. Then he will pour in some water from another glass; but with this strange result—there will be less water in the first glass when he is through than there was when he started!

To accomplish this seeming impossibility, fill the first glass almost to the brim. Then put some water in the second glass, and dash it into the nearly-filled first glass. You will actually transfer the contents of the second glass into the first; but the force of the water will dash out water from the first glass and it will contain less water than when you started.

The trick should be performed on a tray.

3. POURING SMOKE

The trick of pouring smoke from one glass to another is quite surprising; in fact, if it is done well, the smoke will act almost as a liquid.

The glasses should both be wet. Then puff some cigar smoke into one glass, very slowly and gently. The smoke will settle and will fill the glass.

Carefully pour the smoke from one glass to another, doing it very slowly and easily. Be sure to avoid all drafts, and you will discover that the trick is not at all difficult.

4. NON–BREAKABLE GLASS

The magician pushes a tumbler off the edge of table. It falls to the floor, but it does not break!

Practice this with a pillow. Push the glass slowly to the edge of the table and let it topple off. It will turn over in falling, and will strike on the rim. This absorbs the force of the blow, and the glass will not break—as it probably would if it struck the floor on its side.

Of course a delicate glass should not be used. A cheap and fairly thick glass is the kind to do this trick with.

TUMBLER TRICKS

5. A SURPRISING DETECTION

A tumbler is used in this trick—but its sole purpose is to draw attention from the true secret.

An object is laid on the table. The magician leaves the room, and someone pockets the object.

When he comes back, the magician inverts a tumbler on the table and asks each person to touch the bottom of the glass with his or her forefinger. When everyone has done so, the magician looks at the glass and names the person who has the object.

A confederate helps the magician. Not a word is spoken. The confederate, however, knows who took the object, and he waits until that person has touched the glass. Then the confederate touches the glass. The magician knows that the person who touched the glass just before is the one who holds the object.

6. LIFTING SIX GLASSES

The magician states that he can lift six glasses at once, with one hand. That sounds very difficult, and everyone wants a demonstration.

The method is this: arrange five glasses in a circle with the sixth glass in the center. Put a finger in each of four glasses and the thumb in the fifth. Then lift, and as you do so, press the glasses together. The pressure of the five glasses will hold the sixth, and you can lift them all at once.

7. THE NON–FALLING GLASS

Set a glass of water on the table, with a handkerchief spread out beneath it.

Seize the handkerchief, give it a sudden pull, and it will come away, leaving the glass of water standing there.

This trick is not difficult; but it must be performed boldly. Pull the handkerchief straight out, with a quick, steady jerk.

The weight of the water in the glass makes the trick easier, as it holds the glass steady.

8. THE MAGNETIC TUMBLER

The magician takes a glass and turns it over on the table. He places his hand upon it, and lifts. The glass comes with his hand, as though magnetized.

The glass used in the trick should have a depressed bottom. Moisten the bottom of the glass, and set the palm against it, giving the palm a twist. The suction created will enable the hand to lift the glass.

Any glass may be lifted by burning a small piece of paper in it, and then pressing the palm flat upon the brim. This makes it possible to lift the glass with the palm.

9. THE MYSTIC POINTER

A tumbler plays a very important part in this trick.

A small piece of paper is cut in the form of a cross, and is folded slightly in the center of each arm. A needle is placed in a cork, which is stood upright, and the paper cross, which has one arm slightly pointed, is balanced on the needle.

A tumbler is inverted over the small contrivance, and the object is to make the pointer turn in any desired direction.

To do this, rub the outside of the glass with a handkerchief, and you can make the pointer turn. It can be made to revolve by rubbing the handkerchief rapidly around the outside of the glass.

10. THE TOP OF THE TUMBLER

The magician turns a tumbler upside down and lays a coin upon it. He hands a person two matches, and states that it will be impossible for the person to pick up the coin with the two matches and lift it from the top of the tumbler.

The feat looks so easy that the person immediately accepts the challenge. He picks up the coin with the two matches and triumphantly lifts it from the glass.

Then the magician quietly informs him that he has picked up the coin, but he took it from the *bottom* of the tumbler, and not from the top. Hence he has failed to fulfill the necessary conditions of the trick.

11.   GLASS BALANCED ON PLATE

This appears to be an extraordinary feat of juggling. A plate is held in the right hand and the left hand sets a glass on top of the plate. The glass balances there, until it finally topples off and is caught.

The spectators think this trick is difficult, because they see it from in front. The right hand grips the plate on the right side, with the fingers in front. The right thumb is free in back of the plate, and it is extended upward. Thus the glass is set so its base is partly on the plate and partly on the extended thumb, which makes the balancing a simple matter.

12.   THE BALANCED TUMBLER

Take a tumbler, partly filled with water, and try to balance it half way between the horizontal and the perpendicular. Impossible? Not if you know the trick!

Under the tablecloth, place a match-stick. By bracing the bottom edge of the glass against the hidden match, you can effect a precarious balance.

It is advisable to make away with the match-stick after the trick. One method is to "accidentally" spill a few drops of water, and then quickly put a napkin under the table cloth to prevent the water from going through. In removing the napkin, take away the match. Another way is to have a thread attached to the match. Simply pull the thread, and away comes the match.

13. THE TRAVELING GLASS

The Vanishing Glass is a dinner-table trick par excellence; ye' many amateur magicians have neglected it because they were not acquainted with the subtle points that make the trick so effective. The Traveling Glass, performed in the following manner, will prove to be an astonishing mystery.

The magician lays a coin on the table, and sets a glass on the coin. He covers the glass with a piece of newspaper, shaping the paper to fit the glass. He lifts the paper and the glass, and expresses surprise to see that the coin is still there. He covers the coin again, but once more the coin fails to disappear.

The coin is covered with the glass and paper for the third time, and the magician requests two persons to hold the edges of the paper. He holds his right hand over the glass; then rising suddenly, he brings his fist down upon the covered tumbler. The paper collapses. The glass has disappeared!

Then the magician unbuttons the top button of his vest, and extracts the missing glass!

The trick is usually performed with an empty tumbler but a small quantity of water can be used in the glass.

The magician has a napkin in his lap. The second time he lifts the glass from the coin, he looks intently at the coin, and his hand carries the glass to the edge of the table, where the glass is allowed to fall into the lap. The paper retains the shape of the glass and it is replaced on the coin.

As the magician poises his right hand over the paper, his left hand pushes the glass up under the vest. Rising, he strikes the paper, and the left hand pushes the glass further up to the top of the vest.

14. THE GLASS AND THE HAT

This is another dinner-table trick, which is not difficult, but which requires nerve.

The magician asks for a felt hat. He lays the hat on the table and puts a coin alongside of it. He puts the hat over the coin, and waves his left hand above it; but when the hat is lifted, the coin is still there.

The magician sets the hat over the coin, and again waves his left hand. He lifts the hat slightly, but the coin is still there. So he replaces the hat and waves his right hand. This time, when the hat is lifted, a full tumbler of water has appeared beneath it!

The tumbler of water is previously placed on the seat of the performer's chair, alongside of his right knee. The coin is laid on the table, and covered with the hat. The left hand is waved; then it lifts the hat, by taking hold of the crown. The left hand carries the hat to the edge of the table. At the same time the right hand, which has been resting in the lap, lifts the glass of water up into the hat, where the left hand grips it through the crown.

To draw attention from this procedure, the magician leans forward, looks at the coin in amazement, and exclaims: "What! Still there!" The withdrawal of the hat is a perfectly natural movement, and is never suspected, provided that the hands do not fumble.

The left hand replaces the hat and glass over the coin. When the hat is lifted the second time the glass is picked up with it, through the crown. Then the hat and glass are replaced; the right hand lifts the hat and reveals the glass.

CHAPTER XXVI

WATCH TRICKS

1. THE STOP WATCH

A watch is shown, with the second hand running. Anyone can hear the watch tick. But when the watch is laid on the table, it stops immediately.

Method: Have a magnet concealed under the table-cloth. When the watch is laid above the magnet, the works will be stopped. *Never* perform this trick with an expensive watch, as the magnet may affect it. Use an old, cheap watch; especially one that is an erratic time keeper.

2. NUMBER SIX

This is a catch, rather than a trick.

Ask a person the time, and when he replaces his watch in his pocket, mention that although he has been looking at his watch every day, he cannot tell you whether the number six on the face is a Roman numeral (VI) or an Arabic numeral (6).

Of course he will say that he does know; and when he has stated which it is, tell him to look at his watch. To his surprise he will find that there is no number six at all!

The reason is because the second hand of the watch occupies the space provided for number 6. When you ask him for the time your purpose is to learn whether or not his watch has a second hand. If it has one, you may go ahead safely.

WATCH TRICKS

3. TELLING THE TIME

Borrow a watch and tell the company to set it at any time they choose, as five, ten, fifteen (or some other unit of five) minutes after an hour. You leave the room while this is being done, and the watch is laid face down on the table.

When you return, you merely look at the back of the watch and immediately tell the time at which it is set!

Method: You must have a confederate for this trick. You and he divide the table into twelve imaginary squares, each square representing an hour. After the watch has been set and placed on the table, the confederate carelessly moves it into the proper square to designate the hour. At the same time he turns the watch so that the stem points to the minute, imagining that there is a dial around the watch.

One glance at the watch will tell you the time at which it is set.

4. THE MYSTIC ALARM CLOCK

This is a similar trick with an alarm clock; but no confederate is needed. Some person is invited to set the minute hand of the clock at any number he chooses, and to lay the clock face down. Looking at the back of the clock, you name the number to which the large hand points.

Method: The winding knob of an alarm clock often has a little mark which points to the top of the clock when the minute hand points to twelve. If no such mark appears, set the clock at twelve and make a scratch on the knob. When you look at the knob it will tell you where the minute hand is pointing; for the scratch on the knob will act as an indicator on a tiny imaginary dial. The "dial" will be in reverse order, running 12, 11, 10, 9, 8, 7, 6, etc.

5. THE WATCH FROM THE HANDKERCHIEF

A watch is placed in the center of a large handkerchief. The corners of the handkerchief are drawn through a metal ring, and the corners are held by different persons. Then you throw a napkin over the handkerchief, and reaching beneath, immediately draw out the watch!

Method: Although the corners of the handkerchief are held, and the watch cannot pass through the metal ring, the removal of the watch is an easy matter. Take hold of the side of the handkerchief and pull it down through the ring, thus making a space between the corners through which you may withdraw the watch. If you have a coin in your hand, you can drop it in the handkerchief instead of the watch. Then pull the ring down against the coin.

6. DOWN THE SLEEVE

Magicians are supposed to put objects "up their sleeves." In this trick you deliberately drop a watch in your sleeve, and then challenge anyone to find it. The sleeve is shaken, and felt, but no trace of the watch remains!

Method: The watch is apparently put in the left sleeve. Hold your left hand against your face so that the opening of the sleeve comes directly in front of the left breast pocket. Hold the watch between your right thumb and forefinger, and as the other fingers spread the sleeve open, let the watch drop in the pocket. The illusion is perfect. Extend your hand, and shake the sleeve a bit, and everyone will look there for the watch.

7. TAP THE DIAL

The magician lays a watch on the table and tells a person to select any number on the dial, mentally. Taking a pencil, the magician states that he will tap various numbers at random. With the first tap, the spectator is to start counting with the number that he mentally selected.

For instance, if the person chose six, he is to count: six, seven, eight, nine and so on as he hears each pencil tap. He can either turn away and let others watch the tapping, or he can observe the process if preferred. In either case, when he reaches twenty in his count, the person is to say "Stop!"

Not until then does the spectator say a word, his whole count beginning with the chosen number, being entirely mental. At the word "Stop!" the magician's pencil will be resting on the very number that the spectator selected.

The whole process is practically automatic. The performer makes his first eight taps at random, anywhere on the dial, but the next—the ninth tap—is made on Number Twelve. From then on, the performer must tap around the dial counterclockwise; that is to the left: Eleven, ten, nine and so on. The count will always strike the chosen number at twenty.

Instead of a watch, a clock-dial may be used in this trick.

MELVIN POWERS SELF-IMPROVEMENT LIBRARY

ASTROLOGY

BRIDGE

BUSINESS, STUDY & REFERENCE

CALLIGRAPHY

CHESS & CHECKERS

___ CHESS TACTICS FOR BEGINNERS Edited by Fred Reinfeld 10.00
___ HOW TO WIN AT CHECKERS Fred Reinfeld 7.00
___ 1001 BRILLIANT WAYS TO CHECKMATE Fred Reinfeld 10.00
___ 1001 WINNING CHESS SACRIFICES & COMBINATIONS Fred Reinfeld 10.00

COOKERY & HERBS
___ CULPEPER'S HERBAL REMEDIES Dr. Nicholas Culpeper 5.00
___ FAST GOURMET COOKBOOK Poppy Cannon 2.50
___ HEALING POWER OF HERBS May Bethel 5.00
___ HEALING POWER OF NATURAL FOODS May Bethel 7.00
___ HERBS FOR HEALTH—HOW TO GROW & USE THEM Louise Evans Doole 7.00
___ HOME GARDEN COOKBOOK—DELICIOUS NATURAL FOOD RECIPES Ken Kraft 3.00
___ MEATLESS MEAL GUIDE Tomi Ryan & James H. Ryan, M.D. 4.00
___ VEGETABLE GARDENING FOR BEGINNERS Hugh Wilberg 2.00
___ VEGETABLES FOR TODAY'S GARDENS R. Milton Carleton 2.00
___ VEGETARIAN COOKERY Janet Walker 10.00
___ VEGETARIAN COOKING MADE EASY & DELECTABLE Veronica Vezza 3.00

GAMBLING & POKER
___ HOW TO WIN AT POKER Terence Reese & Anthony T. Watkins 10.00
___ SCARNE ON DICE John Scarne 15.00
___ WINNING AT CRAPS Dr. Lloyd T. Commins 10.00
___ WINNING AT GIN Chester Wander & Cy Rice 10.00
___ WINNING AT POKER—AN EXPERT'S GUIDE John Archer 10.00
___ WINNING AT 21—AN EXPERT'S GUIDE John Archer 10.00
___ WINNING POKER SYSTEMS Norman Zadeh 10.00

HEALTH
___ BEE POLLEN Lynda Lyngheim & Jack Scagnetti 5.00
___ COPING WITH ALZHEIMER'S Rose Oliver, Ph.D. & Francis Bock, Ph.D. 10.00
___ DR. LINDNER'S POINT SYSTEM FOOD PROGRAM Peter G Lindner, M.D. 2.00
___ HELP YOURSELF TO BETTER SIGHT Margaret Darst Corbett 10.00
___ HOW YOU CAN STOP SMOKING PERMANENTLY Ernest Caldwell 5.00
___ NATURE'S WAY TO NUTRITION & VIBRANT HEALTH Robert J. Scrutton 3.00
___ NEW CARBOHYDRATE DIET COUNTER Patti Lopez-Pereira 2.00
___ REFLEXOLOGY Dr. Maybelle Segal 7.00
___ REFLEXOLOGY FOR GOOD HEALTH Anna Kaye & Don C. Matchan 10.00
___ YOU CAN LEARN TO RELAX Dr. Samuel Gutwirth 5.00

HOBBIES
___ BEACHCOMBING FOR BEGINNERS Norman Hickin 2.00
___ BLACKSTONE'S MODERN CARD TRICKS Harry Blackstone 7.00
___ BLACKSTONE'S SECRETS OF MAGIC Harry Blackstone 7.00
___ COIN COLLECTING FOR BEGINNERS Burton Hobson & Fred Reinfeld 7.00
___ ENTERTAINING WITH ESP Tony 'Doc' Shiels 2.00
___ 400 FASCINATING MAGIC TRICKS YOU CAN DO Howard Thurston 10.00
___ HOW I TURN JUNK INTO FUN AND PROFIT Sari 3.00
___ HOW TO WRITE A HIT SONG AND SELL IT Tommy Boyce 10.00
___ MAGIC FOR ALL AGES Walter Gibson 10.00
___ PLANTING A TREE TreePeople with Andy & Katie Lipkis 13.00
___ STAMP COLLECTING FOR BEGINNERS Burton Hobson 3.00

HORSE PLAYERS' WINNING GUIDES
___ BETTING HORSES TO WIN Les Conklin 10.00
___ ELIMINATE THE LOSERS Bob McKnight 5.00
___ HOW TO PICK WINNING HORSES Bob McKnight 5.00
___ HOW TO WIN AT THE RACES Sam (The Genius) Lewin 5.00
___ HOW YOU CAN BEAT THE RACES Jack Kavanagh 5.00
___ MAKING MONEY AT THE RACES David Barr 7.00

MELVIN POWERS MAIL ORDER LIBRARY

METAPHYSICS & NEW AGE

RECOVERY

SELF-HELP & INSPIRATIONAL

___NEVER UNDERESTIMATE THE SELLING POWER OF A WOMAN Dottie Walters 7.00
___PRINCESS WHO BELIEVED IN FAIRY TALES Marcia Grad 10.00
___PSYCHO-CYBERNETICS Maxwell Maltz, M.D. 10.00
___PSYCHOLOGY OF HANDWRITING Nadya Olyanova 10.00
___SALES CYBERNETICS Brian Adams 10.00
___SECRET OF SECRETS U.S. Andersen 10.00
___SECRET POWER OF THE PYRAMIDS U.S. Andersen 7.00
___SELF-THERAPY FOR THE STUTTERER Malcolm Frazer 3.00
___STOP COMMITTING VOICE SUICIDE Morton Cooper, Ph.D. 10.00
___SUCCESS CYBERNETICS U.S. Andersen 10.00
___10 DAYS TO A GREAT NEW LIFE William E. Edwards 3.00
___THINK AND GROW RICH Napoleon Hill 10.00
___THINK LIKE A WINNER Walter Doyle Staples, Ph.D. 15.00
___THREE MAGIC WORDS U.S. Andersen 12.00
___TREASURY OF COMFORT Edited by Rabbi Sidney Greenberg 10.00
___TREASURY OF THE ART OF LIVING Edited by Rabbi Sidney Greenberg 10.00
___WHAT YOUR HANDWRITING REVEALS Albert E. Hughes 4.00
___WINNING WITH YOUR VOICE Morton Cooper, Ph.D. 10.00
___YOUR SUBCONSCIOUS POWER Charles M. Simmons 7.00

SPORTS

___BILLIARDS—POCKET • CAROM • THREE CUSHION Clive Cottingham, Jr. 10.00
___COMPLETE GUIDE TO FISHING Vlad Evanoff 2.00
___HOW TO IMPROVE YOUR RACQUETBALL Lubarsky, Kaufman & Scagnetti 5.00
___HOW TO WIN AT POCKET BILLIARDS Edward D. Knuchell 10.00
___JOY OF WALKING Jack Scagnetti 3.00
___RACQUETBALL FOR WOMEN Toni Hudson, Jack Scagnetti & Vince Rondone 3.00
___SECRET OF BOWLING STRIKES Dawson Taylor 5.00
___SOCCER—THE GAME & HOW TO PLAY IT Gary Rosenthal 7.00
___STARTING SOCCER Edward F Dolan, Jr. 5.00

TENNIS LOVERS' LIBRARY

___HOW TO BEAT BETTER TENNIS PLAYERS Loring Fiske 4.00
___PSYCH YOURSELF TO BETTER TENNIS Dr. Walter A. Luszki 2.00
___TENNIS FOR BEGINNERS Dr. H.A. Murray 2.00
___WEEKEND TENNIS—HOW TO HAVE FUN & WIN AT THE SAME TIME Bill Talbert . . . 3.00

WILSHIRE PET LIBRARY

___DOG TRAINING MADE EASY & FUN John W. Kellogg 5.00
___HOW TO BRING UP YOUR PET DOG Kurt Unkelbach 2.00
___HOW TO RAISE & TRAIN YOUR PUPPY Jeff Griffen 5.00

LIBROS EN ESPAÑOL

___CARISMA——CÓMO LOGRAR ESA MAGIA ESPECIAL Marcia Grad 10.00
___CÓMO ALRAER LA BUENA SUERTE A.H.Z. Carr 10.00
___EL CABALLERO DE LA ARMADURA OXIDAD Robert Fisher 10.00
___EL CABALLERO DE LA ARMADURA OXIDAD (con cubierta gruesa) Robert Fisher . . . 20.00
___LA PRINCESA QUE CREÍA EN CUENTOS DE HADAS Marcia Grad 10.00

Available from your bookstore or directly from Melvin Powers.
Please add $2.00 shipping and handling for each book ordered.

Melvin Powers
12015 Sherman Road
No. Hollywood, California 91605

For our complete catalog, visit our Web site at http://www.mpowers.com.